a woman by

God's Grace

Anna Mary Byler

Vision Publishers
Harrisonburg, Virginia

First Edition 1992
Second Printing 1994
Third Printing 1995
Fourth Printing 1996
Fifth Printing 1999
Second Edition 2002
Third Edition 2007

A Woman by God's Grace - ISBN:1-932676-12-0

Attempt has been made to secure permission for the use of all copyrighted material. We have reason to believe some of the included poems were written in the early nineteenth century and, therefore, are in public domain. We welcome any information that will help rectify any needed reference or credits. It will be our privilege to make any adjustments in future editions.

Unless otherwise noted, all Scripture references are from the King James Version of the Holy Bible.

Published by Vision Publishers
Harrisonburg, Virginia

Cover Design: Lonnie Yoder

For additional copies or comments write to:
Vision Publishers
P.O. Box 190
Harrisonburg, VA 22803
Phone: 877/488-0901
or Fax 1-540-437-1969
E-mail: visionpubl@ntelos.net
(see order forms in back)

Anyone wishing to write the author may do so at:
1200 Cold Springs Road
Stuarts Draft, VA 24477

Table of Contents

In an Ideal Christian Family 5
I Need You, God..6
Writer's Acknowledgments 7
Preface...9
Introduction 11

O for a Heart..14
Chapter 1: A Heart—Prepared, Perfect, Purposeful...........15

My Bible 22
Chapter 2: Daily Manna 23

Slow Me Down, Lord 28
Chapter 3: Chew Your Food Well..29

No Life Is Lived in Vain... 32
Chapter 4: All, All, All 33

Christ in the Home.. 38
Chapter 5: Family Altar—the Center of the Home...................... 39

A Husband's Prayer.. 44
Chapter 6: Husband—the Umbrella 45

Prayer in the Kitchen 50
Chapter 7: A True Counterpart 51

My Family Follows Me... 56
Chapter 8: Follow the Leader.. 57

Now.. 62
Chapter 9: Home—Order or Disorder? 63

Parents' Prayer... 68
Chapter 10: Children—Strength or STRESS 69

He Leadeth Me..76
Chapter 11: Reflex of Obedience....................................77

Teach Me 80
Chapter 12: Yoked or Tied?..81

Life's Challenge..84
Chapter 13: Noticed or Noble? 85

Marriage Takes Three...90
Chapter 14: God's Hedge of Protection..........................91

Caring for Each Other...100
Chapter 15: Termites in Marriage 101

God's Will for You and Me...108
Chapter 16: God's Perfect or Permissive Will...............109

A Family Prayer..114
Chapter 17: Love Without a "Net" 115

Abide in Me...120
Chapter 18: Prepare for the Rainy Day.........................121

Don't Quit 126
Chapter 19: Finding the Solution 127

What God Has Given Me 130
Chapter 20: Living in the Basement..............................131

Rules for Daily Living...136
Chapter 21: Walk the Chalk Line!.................................137

Kitchen Prayer 142
Chapter 22: Gather up the Fragments 143

The Joys of a Mother...146
Chapter 23: The Joy of Housecleaning 147

A Mother From A-Z..154
Chapter 24: Retracing My Steps 155

When I Have Time 160
Chapter 25: Working Myself Out of a Job.....................161

Looking for the Sunrise 169

In an ideal Christian family ...

C hrist is given first place.

H appiness prevails.

R ejoicing is heard instead of complaints.

I nterruptions don't destroy family peace.

S torms strengthen a family's love.

T ears and disappointments are shared openly.

I n difficult times, everyone is drawn closer to God.

A visitor always feels welcome.

N eeds of others come before our own needs.

F ussing is not heard.

A time of separation does not sever strong family ties.

M oney is kept in proper perspective.

I nterest is shown equally in every family member.

L ove covers the faults in others.

Y oung people respect and obey their parents.

—Shirley Byler

I Need You, God

Dear God, I do not want to know
What things there are in store
But I implore your help to live
And to accomplish more.
Your hand alone can lead me through
The darkness of the night
And bless me with encouragement
To keep on doing right.
I try to be prepared each day
To take my life in stride . . .
But I need grace to guide my steps
And never leave Your side.
Almighty God, in every thought
I most sincerely pray
For just enough assistance now
That I may never stray.
Be with me every morning when
The sky is gray or blue
And let me find the stars at night
That light the way to you.

Courtesy of Baxter Lane Company, Amarillo, TX, 1975.
Used by permission.

Writer's Acknowledgments

"Now therefore let it please thee to bless the [writing] of thy servant . . . for thou blessest, O LORD, and it shall be blessed for ever" (1 Chronicles 17:27).

I am deeply indebted to . . .

. . . my loving heavenly Father who *"called me by his grace"*.[1] Grace is described as love that stoops. I have experienced God's mercy as He stooped to extend His wonderful grace to me. For that reason I am what I am.

. . . Bennie, my dear husband, who took time from his busy schedule once again to read my scrawls. I desire this book to be an extension and reflection of his ministry.

. . . my loving children:

Sue, for her encouragement and help in typing.

Sharon, for her talent in doing the calligraphy. She is married to Kenneth Troyer, and they have four children: Vincent, Victoria, Dwight, and Thelma.

Shirley, for suggesting the candle and Bible picture. She also helped with the typing.

Steve, Rosa, and their children, Douglas, Margaret, Helen, Katherine, William, and Charles, who have returned from pioneering an Anabaptist church in Ireland. They are currently assisting Steve's father in the family business. On March 3,

1996, Steve was ordained deacon in the Pilgrim Church near Stuarts Draft, Virginia.

. . . Anita Yoder for cheerfully giving many hours to type the manuscript.

. . . Dan Yoder, Ervin Hershberger, Linda Rose Miller, David Miller, Paul Miller, Lavina Gingerich, and others who proofread the manuscript.

. . . those of Pilgrim Church who permitted me to use some illustrations and experiences and to those who encouraged and prayed.

I, as a writer, acknowledge my humanity. I have meant to be fair, accurate, and truthful in all my writing. I am also aware of my unworthiness, but I humbly believe I also know something about the worthiness of an all-sufficient Savior and of the wonderful grace of God who is worthy of all glory and praise.

It was the writer of Proverbs who acknowledged that it is the godly woman's candle that gives light during the night. Even if my candle is but a small light, it is my prayer that there may be those who can light their candle by its flame.

May this feeble attempt articulate the powerful truths of the Scripture and give insight and encouragement to all who desire to become *A Woman by God's Grace*.

"That they may know that this is thy hand; that thou, Lord, *hast done it"* (Psalm 109:27).

---

1. Galatians 1:5

Preface

*E*ach time a baby girl is born, a lifetime of choices is begun. She will grow to become either like the submitted and beautiful Bride of Christ or like the proud and rebellious harlot of Babylon.

In all of God's creation, what is more lovely and attractive than the woman who permits the grace of God to radiate through her life the purity, the humility, the softness that God intended for the female gender? On the contrary, what is less attractive or desirable than a dirty, loudmouthed, selfish, and bossy woman? Considering the great contrast between these two, what is it that determines which description best fits your life? Is it not, in essence, your response to the grace of God?

The Bible contains the mind of God and reveals His marvelous love and grace for all humanity. To the degree that any individual accepts the truth of God's Word in a personal, life-changing way, that person's life will radiate the love and beauty that comes from God.

The feminist movement of our generation has been preaching a different message: the message that women must become more assertive and independent, demanding their rights. This doctrine is self-seeking, rejecting the plan and purpose of God. And what are the results? We are witnessing a society that is crumbling at the very foundation, seemingly spinning totally out of control.

Will we come back to God's way before it is too late? We may not be able to control or decide what others will do, but each one of us decides what course we will take. This is not a once-for-all choice, but many small decisions that are made throughout each day.

That's what this book is all about—reminding and encouraging you, the reader, to set the right priorities and to make wise choices in your everyday life and responsibilities. May the Spirit of God warm your heart and draw you to Himself, that His grace may permeate your life, making it beautiful for Him!

—Dan and Barbara Yoder

Introduction

$\mathcal{G}$race is defined as unmerited, undeserved favor with God. This is the exchange that God gives when self ends at Calvary. The wonderful grace of God transforms a sinner into a saint. It makes duty a delight. Titus 2:11 reminds us that *"the grace of God . . . hath appeared to all* [people]."

It is this grace that makes it possible for our *hearts* to be His *prepared* dwelling place, *perfect and purposeful.* It is the grace of God that gives daily strength through *daily manna* whereby we can live victoriously. The family now can experience worship each day, which reminds each one of whose we are and whom we serve. The *husband* can then be an *umbrella of security* for his wife and children. The wife can become a *true counterpart,* and the children can grow up to be a *strength rather than a stress.* The grace of God directs the husband so he can *follow the leader,* Christ. The whole family knows where they are going because heaven is their goal. The grace of God is that *hedge of protection* as the family meets God's commandments and requirements. *Termites* may try to invade the home, but they are conquered before crucial damage is done.

It is the grace of God that points to God's truth for answers when problems arise. Therefore, we are able to *find the solution* for our problems because we are not satisfied to go around in circles. His grace enables us to mature and become more Christlike. The grace of God does not allow us to *live in the basement* of our spiritual life, but instead, we will feed our spiritual life, so we become a complete person in Christ. In such a condition, we are able to love our spouse and children *without a "net,"* because of our concern that each one grows to become all God has planned for their lives.

God's grace discerns what is *noble* and what pleases God rather than desiring to be noticed. Because we now live unto God, we find His yoke easy and His burden light. Therefore, we are *prepared for the rainy days* that are sure to come. We will not lament the fact that our life is fearful and unfulfilled.

God's grace makes it a privilege to *walk the chalk line* of God's truth, since it is the truth that makes us free. We count it a blessing to *gather up the fragments,* rather than to desire that all our belongings must be either new or the best in quality.

By God's grace we enjoy our children when they demand all of our attention with little or no appreciation. Later in life we can *reflect back* with fond memories and few regrets. Then, as they grow older, our children will still need us as mothers, but not to the extent they did when younger. Meanwhile, we will find *joy in housecleaning.* Although we are *working ourselves out of a job,* by His grace we will find continual fulfillment in following the Shepherd, knowing there are other blessings in store for the faithful woman.

Since her *"candle goeth not out by night,"*[1] her influence continues on even after she has passed from this life. It is then that the wonderful grace of God will usher the faithful woman into His presence, because she was *A Woman for God's Glory, A Woman by God's Grace.*

—Anna Mary Byler

---

1. Proverbs 31:18.

William Carey's lifelong motto:

Expect great things from a great God.
Attempt great things for a great God.

O for a Heart

O for a heart that is whiter than snow!
Kept, ever kept, 'neath the life-giving flow;
Cleansed from all passion, self-seeking and pride,
Washed in the fountain of Calvary's tide.

O for a heart that is whiter than snow!
Calm in the peace He loves to bestow;
Daily refreshed by the heavenly dews,
Ready for service whene'er He shall choose.

O for a heart that is whiter than snow!
With the pure flame of the Spirit aglow;
Filled with a love that is true and sincere,
Love that is able to banish all fear.

O for a heart that is whiter than snow!
Then in His grace and His knowledge to grow;
Growing like Him who my pattern shall be,
Till in His beauty my King I shall see.

O for a heart that is whiter than snow!
Saviour divine, to whom else can I go?
Thou who didst die, loving me so,
Give me a heart that is whiter than snow.

—E. E. Hewitt

Used by permission. Aaron Z. Weaver, 1972.

1

A Heart–Prepared, Perfect, Purposeful

*I*n the seventeenth century, Charles Wesley was inspired to pen the words, "O for a heart to praise my God, a heart from sin set free, a heart that's sprinkled with the blood, so freely shed for me." This illustrates a *prepared heart,* one that is God's dwelling place.

"A heart resigned, submissive, meek, my dear Redeemer's throne; where only Christ is heard to speak, where Jesus reigns alone. A heart in every thought renewed and full of love divine. Perfect, and right, and pure, and good, a copy, Lord, of Thine. An humble, lowly, contrite heart, believing, true, and clean, which neither life nor death can part from Him that dwells within." This describes a *perfect heart.*

"Thy nature, gracious Lord, impart, come quickly from above, write Thy new name upon my heart, Thy new best name of love." This defines a *prepared, perfect, and purposeful heart,* willing to serve God wholeheartedly.

Down through the ages, God spoke and worked through His people. Only those who had prepared their hearts to do God's bidding followed Him closely and carefully. God's eyes

15

"... run to and fro throughout the whole earth, to shew himself strong in the behalf of them whose heart is perfect toward him" (2 Chronicles 16:9a). According to 1 Chronicles 28:9, 10, we are to

> *... know ... the God of thy father, and serve him with a perfect heart and with a willing mind: for the LORD searcheth all hearts ... ; if thou seek him, he will be found of thee...; take heed* [be very careful] *... be strong, and do it.*

Abraham had a prepared heart. In Genesis 17:1b, God said, *"Walk before me, and be thou perfect."* It is interesting to note that Abraham is the first to be called out by God from the generation of Shem, Noah's son. In Genesis 12:2a, God promised Abraham, *"I will make of thee a great nation."* Abraham obeyed and followed God precisely. God looked into Abraham's heart, a heart that desired to please Him. When God spoke, Abraham obeyed. Obedience to God is the first ingredient of a prepared heart. Obedience must be carried out to the finest detail, because God does not overlook any sin when He seeks for a prepared heart as His tabernacle.

Joseph is an outstanding example of one who had a perfect heart. When he was a small boy, his mother died, leaving him without a mother's instruction and encouragement. Because he grew up being his father's favorite, he was often mistreated by his brothers. At 17, he was sold as a slave into Egypt. He was misrepresented, falsely accused, rejected, and even forgotten in prison. All the time God was testing him, and he proved faithful.

Early in life, Joseph's heart was prepared for God's dwelling place. God was preparing him for the promotion of being next to Pharaoh. After these many trials in his life, Joseph was brought from prison to Pharaoh to interpret his dreams. Joseph was quick to recognize God. *"It is not in me: God shall give Pharaoh an answer of peace"* (Genesis 41:16b). This was the secret of Joseph's dedicated life. It is still the same today. If our heart is God's dwelling place and is perfect before God, we too will be quick to acknowledge it is of God and not of man. No wonder Pharaoh said, *"Can we find such a one as this is, a man in whom the Spirit of God is?"* (Genesis 41:38b).

Joseph's life speaks of practical wisdom. He had conviction that did not allow him to commit sin, even though it would cost him years in prison. Instead, he was willing to be falsely accused, leaving his coat in Potiphar's wife's hand.

Daniel is another example of one who prepared his heart and was perfect before God. Therefore, he purposed in his heart to serve God only. Daniel was taken captive as a young man. He met the demands of the king, who was looking for young men who would benefit his kingdom. Even though the king had rules, *"Daniel purposed in his heart that he would not defile himself"* (Daniel 1:8a).

God blessed Daniel as God still blesses people today when they are willing to be counted for Him. In spite of the fact that Daniel was miles from his home and his family, he still purposed in his heart. Because of his obedience, God gave him knowledge and skill in all learning and wisdom.

When the king had a dream, he noted that Daniel could interpret it.[1] The secret of Daniel's success was that *"Daniel blessed the God of heaven, . . . Blessed be the name of God forever and ever"* (Daniel 2:19b, 20a). Later, Daniel again was called by the king to interpret, and immediately he replied, *"But there is a God in heaven that revealeth secrets and maketh known . . ."* (Daniel 2:28a). Much was accomplished because Daniel had prepared his heart and was perfect before God. Therefore, he had a purpose to serve God wholeheartedly.

Obedience to God is the mark of such a heart. To God it is so important that it ranks above all other obedience. We must obey God rather than men. We would be following the best of God's men if we emulated Daniel, Joseph, or Abraham in their example of trust and obedience.

Next to obedience is the desire to please our Maker. When the desire to please is in our hearts, it is accompanied by godly fear. In Exodus 23:27, God says, *"I will send my fear before thee."* God promises protection from the enemy that would hinder our hearts from being perfect before Him. Godly fear must fill our hearts. Proverbs 14:26 says, *"In the fear of the LORD is strong confidence."* When God's fear is part of our heart, we can be holy for God is holy.

We must see and know the exceeding sinfulness of sin[2] in order to get a glimpse of God's holiness. In God's sight, sin is sin; there are none who are less sinful, because our redemption cost the life of God's beloved Son. Solomon tells us it is *". . . the little foxes, that spoil the vines"* (Song of Solomon 2:15b). So it is in our lives. It is those "little things" that we sometimes give different names, such as attitudes, personalities, faults, or weaknesses. These are all sins that hinder our hearts from being pure and perfect tabernacles. All must be confessed and repented of for God to dwell there.

Selfishness and pride are continually in combat with my desire to be Christlike; therefore, I must die to self daily.

Careless speech is a real hindrance. Our words must be *"Yea, yea, Nay, nay: for whatsoever is more than these cometh of evil"* (Matthew 5:37b). *"Let no corrupt communication proceed out of your mouth"* (Ephesians 4:29a). *"How forcible are right words! but what doth your arguing reprove?"* (Job 6:25). *"Death and life are in the power of the tongue"* (Proverbs 18:21a). We must speak *"the truth in love"* (Ephesians 4:15). Like Job, we must pray that God will *"teach me, and I will hold my tongue"* (Job 6:24a). Only God can control and tame that *"unruly evil, full of deadly poison"* (James 3:8b).

Satan uses partial truth as another means of defeating God's prepared dwelling place. *"A double minded man is unstable in all his ways"* (James 1:8). It is human and so easy to agree with everyone and yet not know where we stand. God expects us to be those who *"continue in* [Jesus'] *word."* To such, Jesus says, *"Then are ye my disciples indeed; And ye shall know the truth, and the truth shall make you free"* (John 8:31, 32). God sees right through the dual lifestyle, deep into the heart. There is nothing we can hide from God; therefore, we must bring *"into captivity every thought* [or imagination] *to the obedience of Christ"* (2 Corinthians 10:5). It is so important to *"keep* [our hearts] *with all diligence; for out of it are the issues of life"* (Proverbs 4:23).

Another hindrance to a prepared heart is neglected Bible study and prayer. We must drink deeply and daily to be able to live victoriously. *"Thy word have I hid in mine heart, that I might not sin against thee"* (Psalm 119:11). *"O how love I thy law! It is my meditation all the day"* (Psalm 119:97). It is evident whether we love or tolerate God's Word. In the same measure, we will experience victory or defeat. The saying is very true, "What we feed grows!" So in our devotion to God, when we feed on God's Word, we grow closer to God. When we feed on trash, that is what will spill out at an unguarded moment. God is able to fill our hearts so full of Himself that nothing can come forth but love.

An old illustration is descriptive here: "A cup brimful of

sweet water cannot spill one drop of bitter water, however suddenly jolted." A person must *"study to shew* [himself] *approved unto God, a workman that needeth not to be ashamed, rightly dividing the word of truth"* (2 Timothy 2:15). Our conviction is no deeper than our depth in God's Word; therefore, it behooves all of us to study diligently to know God's will and His way. Conviction is based on God's Word. Preference is based on human reasoning. There is real need to keep a proper balance to maintain conviction and biblical practices.

Materialism robs God of being first in our heart; therefore, trust and faith in God is choked out. We become insensitive to God's still small voice.[3] God placed us in the world, but we are not to be of the world.[4]

For us to be light and salt,[5] our hearts must be God's prepared dwelling. Then His love can radiate through our lives to bring glory to God. *"Set your affection on things above"* (Colossians 3:2a). *"Seek ye first the kingdom of God, and his righteousness"* (Matthew 6:33a). God promises that all our needs shall be supplied. The songwriter says it well: When we get a glimpse of God, "the things of earth will grow strangely dim, in the light of His glory and grace."

Jealousy and envy, even though they may be unnoticed by people, keep our hearts from being God's tabernacles. The antidote for envy is praying for the one who succeeds, rejoicing when he rejoices, and encouraging him to be all God wants him to be. All too often, we desire to be where someone else is and fail in being a prepared heart for God.

God always has answers for our every need. *"Cast away from you all your transgressions, whereby ye have transgressed; and make you a new heart and a new spirit"* (Ezekiel 18:31a). God asks us to make a complete change in our lives. Then our hearts will be new.

I will give them one heart, and I will put a new spirit within you; and I will take the stony heart out of their flesh, and will give them a [pliable] heart of flesh (Ezekiel 11:19, 20).

Then God's plea will be granted: *"O that there were such an heart in them, that they would fear me, and keep all my commandments always"* (Deuteronomy 5:29a). God is still looking for a dwelling place in the tabernacle of our hearts. When we meet God's conditions, He says, *"And there will I meet with thee, and I will commune with thee"* (Exodus 25:22a), in the heart that is prepared, perfect, and purposeful.

---

1. Daniel 2:19.
2. Romans 7:13.
3. 1 Kings 19:12.
4. John 17:16,.
5. Matthew 5:13, 14.

My Bible

When I am tired, the Bible is my bed;
Or in the dark, the Bible is my light.
When I am hungry, it is vital bread;
Or fearful, it is armor for the fight.
When I am sick, 'tis healing medicine;
Or lonely, thronging friends I find therein.

If I would work, the Bible is my tool;
Or play, it is a harp of happy sound.
If I am ignorant, it is my school;
If I am sinking, it is solid ground.
If I am cold, the Bible is my fire;
And it is wings, if boldly I aspire.

Should I be lost, the Bible is my guide;
Or naked, it is raiment rich and warm.
Am I imprisoned, it ranges wide;
Or tempest-tossed, a shelter from the storm.
Would I adventure, 'tis a gallant sea;
Or would I rest, it is a flowerly lea.

Does gloom oppress? The Bible is a sun.
Or ugliness? It is a garden fair.
Am I athirst? How cool its currents run!
Or stifled? What a vivifying air!
Since thus thou givest of thyself to me,
How should I give myself, great Book, to thee!

Courtesy of Back to the Bible Broadcast, Lincoln, NE.
Used by permission.

2

Daily Manna

*I*magine with me, for a few minutes, that we are two little children who left Egypt with the Israelites that night.

We remember hearing the cries of the Egyptians as they found their firstborn dead. We hear our parents say, "Hurry, we must go!"

* * *

We are among the multitude that walked through the Red Sea on dry ground, and we hear our people sing the song of victory when all the Egyptians drowned in the sea.

* * *

We hear our parents talk of all the wonderful works of God. We all bow our heads with theirs in reverence and thanksgiving for His great deliverance.

* * *

As we travel, it gets tiresome and we are weary. The animals are becoming unruly. The babies become fussy, but even so, we must stay on the move.

The day wears on; the sun becomes more pressing and we can hardly keep up with the family. Then we hear our two-year-old say, "Mama, I want to go home. I want my bed." She cheerfully explains that we are going to a new home where we will have plenty of honey and milk and where everything will be pleasant.

* * *

All throughout the camp, people are asking for water. The animals are becoming thirsty, too. In a moment of impatience, someone is heard accusing Moses for bringing the whole group out into the desert to die of thirst. We become fearful! Will we die for lack of water?

But, as before, Moses calls upon God. We catch a glimpse of him on his knees with his hands covering his face, pleading to the great God. God answers his prayer, and soon everyone and every animal has refreshing water to their fill. We hear people rejoicing, but not for long. Fear grips our hearts as we hear grown-ups complaining about the low supply of food. Did we hear correctly? Do they really want to go back to Egypt again? Don't they remember the lashings for not working hard enough?

We look at each other. "Poor Moses," I whisper to my friend, "what is he going to do now?" Sure enough, we see him with his face buried in his hands, down on his knees. He looks like he is crying. We feel like crying too! Don't these grown-ups know how distressing they make it sound for little ears? Once again Moses, now with a shining face, rebukes the complaining people, yet lovingly assures them that God is going to supply their need. *"And in the morning . . . ye shall know that I am the LORD your God"* (Exodus 16:12b).

Manna, fresh manna, the next morning! It is God's miraculous provision for His children. For 40 years God supplied manna, fresh manna, for His children. But like all of God's blessings, there were requirements to meet. They were to gather manna every morning, but if someone tried to gather for the next day, *"it bred worms, and stank"* (Exodus 16:20b).

We, like the Israelites, have left our Egypt. We are on our way to our heavenly Canaan. Far too often, we complain and murmur, but instead, we should plead to God for forgiveness.

Every morning we must receive God's fresh manna, His holy Word. Daily devotion is what we think of as the quiet time with God. This is a must if we are to be victorious. Fidelity is needed in our devotional life, because true faithfulness can be attained only as we draw our strength from heavenly manna. Strength and joy are found in daily meditation as we come to God alone before we meet the duties of the day. Only as we draw from God's limitless grace can we be kept from sinning. We are responsible to keep our lives in order; no one else can do it for us.

Satan knows how very important our personal devotion is in our life; therefore, he is there to hinder or destroy our quiet time with God. Circumstances, situations, or atmosphere are not the real problem. It is self that Satan uses to undermine our effectiveness.

Just as manna in the wilderness lasted only for a day, so in our personal devotion to God His manna gives strength and direction only for that day. Each day we, too, must ask God for a fresh supply.

> *As the hart panteth after the water brooks, so panteth my soul after thee, O God. My soul thirsteth for God, for the living God. . . . When I remember these things, I pour out my soul* (Psalm 42:1, 2a, 4a).

Do I really desire God and search in His Word for strength and refreshment as the deer that has been chased by its enemy and now finally reaches safety and a clear, cool water brook where it drinks long and deeply? So must we also draw strength and courage from God's Word because we, too, are in enemy territory.

Amy Carmichael, in her book *Edges of His Ways*, says it well concerning manna. "First the morning dew fell, then the manna on the dew, then the dew again over the manna."

If this was the way it was for the children of Israel, it wonderfully resembles our daily manna too. First, we pray in quietness, praising and thanking God for who He is. Then we read God's Word (our manna). Next, in thanksgiving, we ask and make our petitions known to Him.

If this is our experience, then the day will be filled with gratitude to our heavenly Father and service to our fellow-man. Throughout each day we will be surrounded by God in quietness and reverence.

The story is told of a lady who went to a famous physician for advice about her ill health. She was a person of nervous temperament. During her visit, she gave the doctor a list of her symptoms. He made a very brief reply: "Go home and read your Bible an hour each day; then come back in a month from today." He dismissed her before she could protest. Anger was her first reaction, but she realized that at least the prescription was not expensive. She determined to read her neglected Bible faithfully. When she went back to her doctor a month later, she seemed like a different person. How did he know what she needed? Pointing to a well-worn and marked open Bible, his reply was, "If we omit daily Bible reading, we lose the greatest force of strength and skill given to us by God."

*Excellence is not sinless perfection,
but rather, a pure heart that desires
to grow in Christ's likeness.*

Slow Me Down, Lord

Slow me down, Lord.

Ease the pounding of my heart by quieting my mind.

Steady my hurried pace with a vision of the eternal reach of time.

Give me, amid the confusion of the day, the calmness of the everlasting hills.

Break the tensions of my nerves and muscles with the soothing music of the singing streams that live in my memory. Help me to know the magical, restoring power of sleep.

Teach me the art of taking minute vacations—of slowing down to look at a flower, to chat with a friend, to pat a dog, to read a few lines from a good book.

Slow me down, Lord, and inspire me to send my roots deep into the soil of life's enduring values, that I may grow toward the stars of my greater destiny.

Courtesy of the Baxter Lane Company, Amarillo, TX, 1975.
Used by permission.

3

Chew Your Food Well!

A young couple and their one-year-old baby were among our guests one Sunday evening. As the mother prepared the food for her little girl to eat, she patted the baby's head and said, "Chew your food well!" It reminded me that my heavenly Father also expects me to chew my food as I meditate and study His word. Only as I partake of His Word and make it a part of my life will His Word be of any benefit to me.

Chewing our food properly is essential for our digestive system. The same is true in our spiritual life. We must read God's Word with a deep love and devotion in our hearts for our Master. Then our minds and our hearts will be open to receive His truth.

With my whole heart have I sought thee: O let me not wander from thy commandments. Thy word have I hid in mine heart that I might not sin against thee (Psalm 119:10, 11).

Many of us have experienced the excitement of a young child eagerly anticipating a good meal. What enthusiasm is shown as the food cools to taste! Does God see eagerness and excitement in my Christian life? Is there enthusiasm when the Bible is read? Does God's Word become a part of my life? Does God see growth in my life?

29

We become very concerned when our little children lose their appetites, or when they are satisfied with only milk. Their growth is stunted. How much more is our heavenly Father concerned that we love Him and enjoy His Word and make it a part of our life! A sluggish spiritual appetite also indicates that we are stunted and sickly, reading little or nothing or reading just because we feel we must.

I like the rendering of Hebrews 5:12-14 and Hebrews 6:1a in *The Living Bible.*[1] It describes this kind of person:

> *You have been Christians a long time now, and you ought to be teaching others, but instead you have dropped back to the place where you need someone to teach you all over again the very first principles of God's Word. You are like babies who drink only milk, not old enough for solid food. And when a person is still living on milk it shows he isn't very far along in the Christian life, and doesn't know much about the difference between right and wrong. He is still a baby-Christian! . . . Let us stop going over the same old ground again and again. . . . Let us go on instead to other things and become mature in our understanding, as strong Christians ought to be.*

Just as we are concerned that babies grow and mature, so much more does God desire for us to grow up. We can grow up and mature in our Christian life only as we feed on God's all-sufficient nourishment.

Our hearts must be renewed and pricked by God.

Now when they heard [these things] *they were pricked in their heart and said . . . what shall we do?* [Peter told them] *Repent . . . and ye shall receive the gift of the Holy Ghost* (Acts 2:37, 38).

In obedience and love to God, we will be sensitive to meet all of God's requirements. As we continue to know God's Word and as we chew our spiritual food well, we will also share with the disciples the Emmaus road experience.

Did not our heart burn within us, while [Jesus] talked with us by the way, and while he opened to us the scriptures? (Luke 24:32b).

Only then can this poem be our testimony:

The Precious Bible

Though the cover is worn
And the pages are torn;
Though places bear traces of tears,
Lots more precious than gold
Is the Book worn and old
That can shatter and scatter my fears.

When I prayerfully look
In the precious old Book,
Many pleasures and treasures I see;
Many tokens of love
From the Father above
Who is nearest and dearest to me.

This old Book is my guide;
It's a friend by my side,
It will lighten and brighten my way.
And each promise I find
Soothes and gladdens my mind,
As I read it and heed it each day.

—Author unknown

---

1. *The Living Bible* (Wheaton, Illinois: Tyndale House Publishers, 1971).

No Life Is Lived in Vain

No one lives in vain for Jesus.
Let this truth sink in your mind
As you labor in His vineyard,
Doing well your work assigned,
Keeping patience through your trials,
Seeking not a place to quit;
Till you are called to come up higher
Where the true and faithful sit.

—Author unknown

"*Therefore, my beloved* [sisters], *be ye stedfast, un-moveable, always abounding in the work of the Lord, forasmuch as ye know that your labour is not in vain in the Lord*" (1 Corinthians 15:58).

4

All, All, All

No ruler or emperor has ever demanded such total dedication as God does. *"Thou shalt love the LORD thy God with **all** thine heart, and with **all** thy soul, and with **all** thy might"* (Deuteronomy 6:5, emphasis added).

It is important that we understand the cost of total dedication or discipleship. When we think of a disciple, we generally think of a learner or a follower. The definition of the Greek word brings out a more meaningful thought: "One who accepts his instruction and makes it the rule of his life." This means commitment to Christ with no reservations.

We may think of ourselves as Christians, but unless we meet the requirements of God, we will find ourselves weighed in a balance and found wanting.[1] Only the one who truly believes is obedient, and only the one who is obedient truly believes.

The following questions test our honesty to the lordship of Christ:

1. Do I accept Jesus' instructions, and is that the rule of my life?

2. Is Jesus Christ on my list of priorities and above any earthly relationship I have?

3. Do I value my commitment to Christ more than I do my selfish ambitions?

4. Is the cross of Jesus a joy? Do I count all else as nothing?

5. Have I forsaken all to follow Christ wholeheartedly?

He that loveth father or mother . . . son or daughter more than me is not worthy of me. And he that taketh not his cross, and followeth after me, is not worthy of me. He that findeth his life shall lose it: and he that loseth his life for my sake shall find it (Matthew 10:37-39).

Discipleship is the heart of the matter and is a matter of the heart. We dare not be careless in our commitment to Christ in our daily living. Every day must be a serious day. Our life is an open book before God. Therefore, it is impossible to hide anything because God sees right into the deepest recesses of our heart. Moses met God at the burning bush.[2] In Exodus 4:2, God asked Moses what he had in his hand. Moses replied, *"A rod."* That was Moses' only possession, and God asked him to cast it upon the ground. It became a serpent, but when God told Moses to pick it up, Moses obeyed. The rod became "God's rod."[3] We, too, must obey God and surrender our only (best-loved) possession, our *all* to the Lord, by casting it at Jesus' feet. Then our life will become a vessel through which God's love flows to our fellowmen.

There is no person as free as the person who has given *all* to the lordship of Christ. *"He that hath the Son hath life; and he that hath not the Son of God hath not life"* (1 John 5:12). To many, the term *"Lord"* has lost its significance. Jesus must be both Lord and Savior, or He is not Lord at *all.*

I have struggled with the realization of what giving *all* to Jesus means. What if He would ask for something that I could not part with? Jesus does not easily give up. He gently probes until we give *all* to the best of our ability. The song "Whatever it takes to draw me closer to You, Lord; that's what I'll be willing to give" has been a challenge to me. Slowly but surely, I know I have nothing but that it first is God's and He has only lent these blessings to me to be enjoyed for a season.

My health has been at stake. I couldn't work or enjoy traveling because of an inner ear problem. So when Bennie needed to travel by air, I knew I had to stay at home. I was not willing to go through all the severe pain and sickness that would last up to a week later.

Our children had goals and we encouraged them to be *all* God wanted them to be, not putting them into the same mold, but rather allowing God to lead them. One chose to go to Belize to teach school for two years. Another served the Lord in Ireland for several years. The third got married and is the busy mother of children. The youngest chose to give her first five years of adulthood working at a counseling center. We don't know what *"all"* may include, but we can trust our God to always choose what is best for us.

Today I know that it is safe to give *all* to Jesus, because of His faithfulness in the past. Giving *all* to Jesus is a process.

Acts 10:13-15 records a conversation Peter had:

And there came a voice to him, Rise, Peter; kill, and eat. But Peter said, Not so, Lord; for I have never eaten any thing that is common or unclean.

"Not so, Lord" is a phrase that should not be found in the genuine Christian's vocabulary. We cannot say "no" and have Jesus as Lord of our life. Either we refuse Jesus' lordship or else Jesus is Lord of all!

1 Corinthians 15:28 says,

And when all things shall be subdued unto him, then

shall the Son also himself be subject unto him that put **all** *things under him, that God may be* **all** *in* **all.**

Surrendering *all* to the lordship of Christ is an individual matter. Surrender means breaking the husk of my stubborn independence to God. It is not having my own ideas, but absolute loyalty and obedience to Jesus. Very few of us know about loyalty for Christ's sake. Not until I deliberately sign away my rights do I become a disciple of Jesus, following carefully and making Him the ruler of my life.

When Jesus is Lord of *all,* He gives a new dimension of love—sacrificial, agape love. The love of God is the highest and deepest love that can prevail. Therefore, when this love is present, husband and wife and family members will know a secure love, a love that is not swayed by circumstances. Since agape love is a selfless love, our love is rooted and settled there. God will also bless with "phileo" or physical love. Since many individuals and families allow self and "phileo" love to be their first concern, their love diminishes. When Christ is Lord, the godly love makes the difference. It is this agape love that enables individuals and couples to become more Christlike because God is their foundation. If Jesus is Lord, then our life is disciplined, structured, and organized day by day as we press toward the goal of godliness, since becoming like Jesus is a process.

One husband said to his wife, "I could not love you half as much if I would not love Jesus most!" For the Christian wife who has surrendered everything to the lordship of Christ, there is no greater security than such a love.

"All, all, all" is so inclusive! According to Matthew 28:18-20, God gives *all* power to live victoriously to those who acknowledge their weakness. His strength knows no limit! He gives unbounded grace to *all* people when *all* things are obeyed. Only then can God's presence, the unceasing fellowship of Christ, be ours alway.

All, all, all alway!

---

1. Daniel 5:27.
2. Exodus 3:1, 2.
3. Exodus 4:17, 20.

Christ in the Home

Give us homes that God has founded, give us homes with
*   love unbounded;*
* Give us homes where Jesus' presence can be felt;*
Give us homes where father, mother, son, and daughter,
*   sister, brother,*
* All in prayer to God the Father oft have knelt.*

Give us homes where faith is treasured; give us homes where
*   joy is measured.*
* By time and the devotion paid the Word;*
Give us homes where love is yearning for the soon returning;
* Give us homes where lives are centered in the Lord.*

—*H. H. Savage*

Courtesy of Back to the Bible Broadcast, Lincoln, NE.
Used by permission.

5

Family Altar—
the Center of the Home

"*O* LORD our Lord, how excellent is thy name in all the *earth!*" (Psalm 8:1a). Can it be said of your home that God is the halo, that God is the luminous radiation of glory that surrounds your life as an individual, and that which surrounds your family?

In order to enjoy the blessings of a family altar, a deep devotion and dedication must be the heartthrob of both parents. As always, God has some requirements too.

1. Our hearts *must* be cleansed from all self-seeking by the blood of Jesus.

2. Our focus *must* be for glorifying God and for the advancement and blessing of our family.

3. All selfish ambition and vanity *must* be brought to Calvary. These tend to bog us down when we bow in prayer in our personal relationship with God.

4. Our soul *must* seek God in everything. This is only found as we meet God on a daily schedule.

Then in such an attitude of personal worship, parents bring into the home the wonderful attribute of the family altar—the daily meeting of God and family.

Ezekiel reminds us in chapter 44:5,

Mark well, and behold with thine eyes, and hear with thine ears all that [God says] *unto thee concerning all the ordinances . . . all the laws . . . mark well the entering . . .* [and the] *going forth. . . .*

Parents are commanded to spell out clearly the boundaries and limits with eyes and ears that take notice, and to see intellectually, giving individual attention to all the commandments and ways of God. Only then will they become a part of their children. God also holds parents responsible concerning the "going and the comings." Even our entrances and exits must bring glory to God.

Ezekiel 41:22b mentions *"the table that is before the Lord."* Exodus 25:30 says, *"And thou shalt set upon the table shewbread before me alway."* Both references describe the tabernacle, a type of our home. God keeps returning to the center point as His dwelling place with His people. This also reminds us that a man lives his whole life in God's divine presence. Worship today is just the same as in Ezekiel's day, a mere form devoid of blessing if our lives are not found in accordance with God's standard of obedience and holiness.

When family worship is in true obedience and holiness, God enables the family to worship Him *"in spirit and in truth."*[1] Just as God was concerned that the tabernacle was holy, without sin, so He is concerned that our family worship is a holy place where the whole family can experience the same glory of the Lord that enabled Ezekiel to see God's glory. It is still God's desire to fill our tabernacle, too, with His presence.

It takes effort to have a meaningful, scheduled family worship, but the value far outweighs the determination that it requires. At times we get the idea that once our children are teenagers it will be easier to be on schedule. Or we reason that we will wait until later. But there is never a better time than now. For babies and small children, family worship can be their "little church" where they learn to sit still and to refrain from loud noises.

Several years ago, we were faced with having one of our girls change jobs. This meant earlier rising or no family devotions and breakfast together. We chose to adapt to her schedule, to get up earlier and have breakfast and family devotions together. We still struggle at times to meet her schedule, but some time ago our daughter told me, "I'll miss breakfast, but I would rather not miss family worship." That was the encouragement we needed again to get our priorities in order.

In the morning before the family goes in various directions, it is such a blessing to gather around a table for breakfast and worship. Someone suggested that the Bible be part of the morning meal. What a blessing to read God's Word and pray for each family member as they face another new day!

There are different ways to make family worship effective. A portion of Scripture can be read by taking turns reading, or else one person can be in charge. Devotional books can provide valuable supplements to stimulate thought and discussion along with the regular Bible reading.

For small children, daily devotions should be simple, brief, and reverent. As children grow older, they can learn to contribute. This is where the parents' private devotions become a blessing and a challenge to their children. Share with the family an outstanding verse that has been a blessing, or ask a question that will stimulate the children's thinking. Perhaps for some families, different hours of the day would better fit their schedule. Some think of sitting in the living room for family worship as being more reverent.

Praying is also very important. Bowing heads is one way, but kneeling is more reverent. Why is it that many people kneel with their backs turned toward each other? We were challenged years ago about praying in such a manner. The suggestion was given to form a circle facing each other. The coffee table in our living room served as the family altar with all of us kneeling around, forming a circle. Standing in a circle holding hands can also be a blessing for a family. Of course, the mode is not so important as worshiping God and pleasing Him.

The phone can be a disturbing factor. Some choose to disconnect it during their worship.

At times a mother finds herself totally responsible for family devotions when her husband is absent or perhaps on a phone call. It has been our conviction that if Bennie is not present, I will take charge. When our children were small, they shared by reading sentences or phrases in the portion we were reading. Sometimes they shared in sentence prayers or led in prayer. As they became older, they took turns choosing a portion to read and made at least one comment. This was planned in advance and did not come as a surprise.

Charles Finney made the comment years ago, "If parents teach and read the Bible without application, this is worse than no teaching at all." The results will bring inevitable injury to the hearers, because truth separated from life is not truth in the biblical sense.

The reason we are to be consistent in family devotions is that this is one way to introduce our children to the Bible way of life. Paul reminds us:

That Christ may dwell in your hearts by faith; that
ye, being rooted and grounded in love, may be able to

comprehend . . . the breadth, and length, and depth, and height; and to know the love of Christ . . . [being] *filled with all the fulness of God* (Ephesians 3:17-19).

A. W. Tozer shared a concern about the difference between present-day people and their forefathers. The forefathers were concerned about the "root of the matter" and present-day people seem concerned only about "the fruit." For that reason, we have an awesome responsibility that we dare not neglect. During family worship, we are silently yet powerfully instilling conviction into the lives of our children. We must be diligent to inspire them with the ideals of God's Word. The Bible is a book of exhortation based upon facts. The greatest portion is devoted to urgent effort to persuade people to alter their ways and to bring their lives into harmony with the will of God.

The proverb "Seeing is believing" is so true in family worship and in our relationship to God in everyday encounters. Therefore, we must be those who not only profess Jesus, but who also possess Christ so *"that we may present* [our children perfectly loyal] *in Christ Jesus"* (Colossians 1:28b).

---

1. John 4:24b.

A Husband's Prayer

Lord, teach me that 60 minutes make an hour, 16 ounces a pound, and 100 cents a dollar. Help me live such a life of integrity that I can lie down at night with a clean conscience. Grant me a wholesome desire to earn an honest living, but deafen me to the jingle of tainted money. Blind me to the faults of my family, but reveal to me my own. Guide me so that each night when I look across the dinner table at my wife I shall have nothing to conceal. Keep me young enough to laugh with little children and sympathetic enough to be considerate of old age. So when I come to the bend in the road and I relive my life, may I be able to take a backward look on life with few regrets. Because I know that "a good name is rather to be chosen than great riches" (Proverbs 22:1a).

6

Husband—the Umbrella

*H*ave you ever seen a man receive a flagrant insult, only to turn a little pale, then give a meek answer? This is the description of a spiritually strong man. Or have you seen a man in anguish stand as if he were carved of solid rock, mastering himself? What about a man bearing the toils of the day, yet never boasting of his endurance. That is strength! He who with strong passions remains chaste, keenly sensitive, with manly powers of indignation in himself, who can be provoked and yet restrain himself and forgive—he is a truly strong man, a spiritual hero.

Consistency, integrity, caution, and a desire to be right carried out in practice are to human character what truth, godly fear, and love are to religion. Such virtues can never be

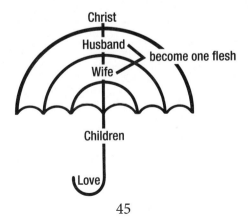

reproached. These are the characteristics of a godly husband who is an umbrella for his wife and children.

God does not require one thing of His children without also giving specific instructions. The Bible has answers to any question we may face.

In Genesis 18:19 God gives a striking testimony of a husband who was a godly leader, and therefore an umbrella: *"I know him* [Abraham], *that he will command his children and his household after him, and they shall keep the way of the* LORD." Abraham followed God carefully and faithfully. He carried out God's plan precisely.

Noah is another example. *". . . Noah found grace in the eyes of the Lord. . . . Noah was a just man and perfect in his generations, and Noah walked with God"* (Genesis 6:8, 9). *"Thus did Noah; according to all that God commanded him, so did he"* (Genesis 6:22). Through Noah's obedience to God, his family was safe and secure during the flood that destroyed every living person except eight souls.[1]

Job is another example of *"a perfect and an upright man, one that feareth God and escheweth evil"* (Job 1:8b). He was a priestly husband, representing his family to God.

> *Job sent and sanctified them, and rose up early in the morning, and offered burnt offerings . . . for Job said, It may be that my sons have sinned. . . . Thus did Job continually* (Job 1:5b).

Even though Job was *"the greatest of all the men in the east,"*[2] he had his priorities straight: God first, his family's spiritual well-being second, then his business. Everything was in its proper place. No wonder Satan was jealous and plagued Job! Job is a noteworthy example for husbands today who are serious about their role.

In John 4:43-54 we read the account of a nobleman who came to Jesus. He pleaded for help because his son was dying. Jesus told the nobleman, *"Go thy way, thy son liveth."* The man returned to his home having faith in Jesus' words. As a result, the son was healed and the nobleman believed, along with his whole house.

Acts 10:2 challenges us with a godly example of a praying husband and father. Cornelius was a centurion, *"a devout man, and one that feared God with all his house, which gave much alms to the people, and prayed to God alway."*

Acts 16:25-34 relates the beautiful story of the conversion of the jailer who was brought to repentance because Paul and Silas prayed and sang praises to God even though they had been cast into the inner prison with their feet made fast in the stocks. The jailer was in the process of committing suicide when Paul cried with a loud voice, *"Do thyself no harm: for we are all here."* The Philippian jailer took the men, washed their stripes, and set meat before them. He rejoiced, believing in God with all his house.

It is an unmatched blessing for the family if the husband is a godly head and leads all the members of his family into the Christian faith. When faith in God becomes the way of life for the head, it is usually shared by the whole family. Because he believes, they all believe. Pardon, peace, and rejoicing are all products of one man taking God's Word seriously.

In order for the husband to be an umbrella for his family, he must be Spirit-controlled. *"Walk in the Spirit, and ye shall not fulfill the lust of the flesh"* (Galatians 5:16b). *"For as many as are led by the Spirit of God, they are the sons of God"* (Romans 8:14). If the husband permits God to lead him, he will not be swayed by mood swings. We dare not be congenial and cheerful when circumstances are right, then critical and curt when situations are the opposite. Moody people do have an effect on others, and husbands have a great influence on those closest to them.

Acts 27:25 portrays Paul as a good example of one who did not allow his moods to fluctuate with circumstances. It had been the fourteenth day of fasting for Paul and the ship crew because of a tempestuous sea. Paul encouraged them, "... *Be of good cheer: for I believe God. . . .*" There is no greater comfort and security than when the husband believes God and acts upon that. Husbands have a great influence in creating stable moods in the home. Irritation and bad moods must be confessed as sin and forsaken. Spiritual fidelity is imperative. As *"iron sharpeneth iron"* (Proverbs 27:17), so God's Spirit must be allowed to polish and beautify the inner life by responding properly in the home.

Just as the umbrella has two positions, so the husband has the choice to be a protection for his family or else be concerned only about himself. Jonah, for example, was controlled by his selfish moods. Instead of obeying God and rejoicing, he pouted and complained (Jonah 4:1-4).

When the husband is an umbrella, his family will have a restful and secure place to live. They are at peace because *"in the fear of the LORD is strong confidence"* (Proverbs 14:26a). The home will be free from friction and confusion because the husband is constantly receiving his direction from his Head, the Lord Jesus. Since friction results from selfishness, no "little sins" are found because the umbrella continually shelters the family from the ever-present worldly surroundings. Contentment and fulfillment reign because their treasures are laid up in heaven.[3] Plenty of spiritual food is always available; therefore, there is no hunger or hankering after the things of this world.

There is no jealousy or envy because all are equal and loved for who they are. Joy and peace are the elements that reign since faithfulness in all things is so important.[4] The ever-living Christ is here to bless. The nearer you live to God, the nearer you will be to each other in your family.

Adapted from material presented by Ray Stutzman, Plain City, OH. Used by permission.
1. Genesis 7:23.
2. Job 1:3.
3. Matthew 6:20.
4. Luke 16:10.

Prayer in the Kitchen

Lord of all pots and pans and things,
Since I've no time to be
A saint by doing lovely things, or
Watching late with Thee,
Or dreaming in the dawnlight, or
Storming heaven's gates,
Make me a saint by getting meals and
Washing up the plates.

Although I must have a Martha's hands,
I have a Mary's mind;
And when I black the boots and shoes,
Thy sandals, Lord, I find.
I think of how they trod the earth
What time I scrub the floor;
Accept this meditation, Lord,
I haven't time for more.

Warm all the kitchen with Thy love, and
Light it with Thy peace.
Forgive me all my worrying, and make
All grumbling cease.
Thou who didst love to give men food,
In room or by the sea,
Accept this service that I do—
I do it unto Thee.

Courtesy of Back to the Bible Broadcast, Lincoln, NE.
Used by permission.

7

A True Counterpart

*H*ow much of the world's success and prosperity is contained in the words of this poem! The power of a wife for good or evil is immense! She makes home the domain of joy and contentment, or joy is altogether unknown. A wife who is a true counterpart to her husband is an encouragement to her family, strengthening them to perform what is right. She gives hope and is an example in endurance. Godly wisdom is in her mouth. She ministers at the very fountain of life and happiness. It is her hand that pours out with an overflowing cup its soul-refreshing waters. Her ardent spirit breathes the breath of life into all enterprises. Her patience and constancy are instrumental in carrying forward to completion the work of God. Her moral sensibility is an unseen power at work to build the family that will bring glory to God and contribute to the church and society. Her hands are trained to intelligence, virtue, and love. She makes her home a place of contentment, a place where her family loves to be.

In creation, God planned that man would subdue the earth, and that woman would be his helper. Together, they would be complete. A *counterpart*, according to Webster, is a "thing that fits another perfectly; one who completes or complements." The first step in becoming a true counterpart is to experience spiritual regeneration. This is a miraculous work of God whereby His Spirit is imparted to us. It marks the beginning of a new life in which we are being conformed daily to the character of our Lord and Savior Jesus Christ.

A true counterpart is more than just a helper. She has chosen the vocation of wife and mother; therefore, she is diligent to learn and grow in all areas of this role. An example could be to work as if one were aiming for the presidency. Proverbs 31:10-31 describes the wonders of a good counterpart. She is a virtuous woman having strength of character. The fear of God is her first concern. Her spirit is one of reverence, and the life she lives is one of worship and adoration to her heavenly Father. She studies daily and diligently to find God's perfect will. She finds contentment at home, since she knows her heart and home are God's sanctuary. Constantly and earnestly are the ways she lives, because she is well aware that the joy and security of her home depend upon the favor and blessing of her heavenly Father. Purity marks her thoughts and actions. She gives her whole heart and life for the sake of her husband and children. She is faithful to God and her family even in the little, unnoticed, and hidden areas of life. This makes her life pure and holy because she has nothing to hide. The true counterpart is tireless in pursuing her responsibilities. Even though she becomes tired physically, she never dreads nor tires of her God-given responsibility.

The virtuous woman has no time for idle talk. She does not nag, nor is her speech degrading. Because she is familiar with the laws of God, she knows the secret of lasting joy. Therefore, she guides her children in God's way and instills heaven-bound wisdom into their minds early in life. Compassion and kindness describe her way of life. By gentleness and encouragement she reaches out to friends and neighbors alike, giving constant comfort and cheer. Since she plans ahead, she is not frustrated when she is faced with interruptions. Instead, she finds joy even in the unpleasant tasks because she views each situation from God's point of view.

Integrity is her watchword, making her honest in all business and personal matters. Strength and dignity are her characteristics. She has an undivided loyalty.

In meekness she stands by her husband, living the truth of God's Word. She is a woman of a meek and quiet spirit. Love and esteem are woven in her character. Her influence is felt more often than recognized, even after her face and voice are no longer seen and heard.

The true counterpart can think of the future and still not worry or be fearful, because she knows God is already there. If she is faithful today, God's grace will be her strength tomorrow. She is faithful in holding the faith of Christ. She lives by His principles and is guided by His Spirit, fulfilling His law of love. Her life is a life of prayer, since she knows that prayer is the key that unlocks the door of God's grace and His manifold blessings.

The true counterpart chooses to be cheerful even though circumstances may not always be ideal. She avoids extremes. "Even-keel" describes her disposition. Because of her diligence at home, her husband is able to minister to other needs and fulfill God's call in church responsibilities at home or abroad.

Forgiveness is another virtue. At times she is misunderstood, envied, or slandered. When these wrongs are confessed to her, she keeps on loving, even though at times it may appear hard to love, since loving is the bond of perfection.[1] The peace of God rules her heart and life; therefore, thanksgiving is her response. God's love flows through her life to others around her, because Jesus' blood has made her a pure and clean channel through which God can bless others.

She is one who gives, and gives, and gives again, with no thought of repayment. Since selfishness for her has ended at Calvary, she has no rights of her own.

God's plan for the virtuous woman is for her to spend her lifetime serving others. The young wife serves her husband and children and later her aging parents. Older women train and assist the younger to pursue motherhood and encourage them when their tasks seem wearisome and endless. Serving from the heart of love makes duty a delight. Since charity begins at home, it is an opportunity and a ministry rather than a profession.

Homemaking is not a meager chore. It is a lifetime commitment. Humble? Yes! But she who humbles herself will be exalted.[2]

Submission is another virtue that has been defined as "to work under and for her head's best interest, in obedience to God." Since a virtuous wife is of strong character, she will have her life in command. Therefore, she will be able to encourage her husband to be all God wants him to be. Even though she is a discreet wife, she will gladly submit to her husband's discretion. He is her final authority under God.

Since she is a virtuous woman, she marks well her bulwarks (is very concerned) about the home because her influence will reach generations to come (Psalm 48:13, paraphrased). Then she claims the following verse: *For this God is our God for ever and ever: he will be our guide even unto death"* (Psalm 48:14).

I was reminded of the dreams and goals I had as a 20-year-old bride. I wanted to be the "thing that fits another perfectly." Now, years later, I regret that I have at times failed my husband.

Still, it is my heartfelt desire to be that true counterpart so he can be the man God has planned for him to be. There have been times when he was discouraged and I could help him pray, tell him I love him, stand by him, and share a verse that God had given me as an encouragement. Some time ago, I was convicted that I had not always spoken kindly and respectfully about others to my husband, and I asked his forgiveness. It is of utmost importance that I be like a refreshing cup of cold water to my husband.

The world is watching, and we dare not disappoint God by refusing to be a true counterpart. If we fail, we are encouraging the world to reject God's Word.[3] What a privilege to be counted worthy by God to live under the commanding influence of God's principles, breathing His Spirit and shedding a Christian influence in our home and in the church community where we live. What is more blessed than doing the most excellent work of God by filling an honorable and useful sphere—that of being a true counterpart.

---

1. Colossians 3:14.
2. Matthew 23:11, 12.
3. Titus 2:5.

My Family Follows Me

A careful man I want to be:
For my family follows me.
I do not dare to go astray
For fear they'll go the selfsame way.

I cannot once escape their eyes;
Whate'er they see me do they try;
Like me they say they're going to be—
For my family follows me.

They think that I am good and fine;
Believe in every word of mine.
The bad in me they must not see—
For my family follows me.

I must remember as I go,
Through summer's sun and winter's snow,
I'm building for the years to be
For my family follows me.

—Author unknown
adapted by Shirley Byler

8

Follow the Leader

*A*s I drove along the interstate, black, fierce clouds indicated that a thunderstorm was approaching. Several minutes later, rain came down in sheets, making it nearly impossible to see the vehicle ahead. The red taillights dimly revealed the car's location and movements. Occasionally, the turn signal would blink, alerting me to change lanes. Taking a glance in the rearview mirror and checking both sides of the car, I carefully maneuvered the car to continue following the vehicle ahead. When we finally arrived at our destination, it was with a grateful heart that I turned off the ignition. I expressed my thankfulness to my heavenly Father and to my husband who had made it as easy as he could for me to follow him.

This incident reminded me of God's order for husband and wife. Husbands are commanded to follow Christ their head and love as He loved the church. Wives are to submit and follow; husbands are to love and lead.

Some years ago, Brother Ervin Hershberger[1] related an account of a bride and groom at their premarital counseling session that has been a challenge to me. He said the bride, with meekness and humility, looked into her future husband's eyes and said, "I will follow you as you follow Christ." What a commitment and what a challenge to search our own lives to see how strong our own commitment is. Since the husband is to follow Christ and the wife is to follow her husband, there will be no competition, rivalry, envy, or strife because the two are content when their eyes are fixed on Jesus.

God expects there to be clear goals and patterns in marriage. If I could not have followed the vehicle my husband was driving by watching the turn signals or brake lights, or if he would have given directions opposite from what he planned, or if he would not have had "home" as our goal, I could not have followed at all.

It is of utmost importance that leaders and followers remain balanced in this world of extremes. We must develop inner strength, godly character, and peace in a world of weakness and uncertainty. If followers are to know how to perform, the leader must know and clearly define the goal or explain what he means. A good leader knows why he does what he does; therefore, he will lead clearly and plainly so it is easy to follow. The Bible tells us in Matthew 15:14, *". . . if the blind lead the blind, both shall fall into the ditch."* In Amos 3:3, we are asked the question, *"Can two walk together, except they be agreed?"*

In order to be worthy of our calling as leaders and followers, we must be sensitive to God's call, to do God's bidding in God's way. This takes a *clear mind: "Let this mind be in you, which was also in Christ Jesus"* (Philippians 2:5).

A *cheerful disposition* is necessary. *"Being filled with the fruits of righteousness . . . unto the glory and praise of God"* (Philippians 1:11).

A *discreet mouth* is also important. *"Set a watch, O LORD, before my mouth; keep the door of my lips"* (Psalm 141:3).

We need *keen judgment* to be able to discern God's will. *"The fear of the LORD is the beginning of wisdom"* (Proverbs

9:10a). To make proper decisions and choose the best, we must keep our hearts *"with all diligence; for out of it are the issues of life"* (Proverbs 4:23b).

Humility is also of great importance. *"Let nothing be done through strife or vainglory; but in lowliness of mind let each esteem other better than themselves"* (Philippians 2:3).

We must continually be aware that our example outlines our profession. Although often unknown to us, there are those who are following our example. Just as leaders train other leaders, we as wives and followers, also are training others by the example of how we follow our leader. This influence will be passed on!

With Psalm 23 as a guide, I have paraphrased the following:

A True Leader

1. The husband is the leader; the wife shall have no unnecessary frustrations.

2. Since he is the "house-band," the bands are security and peace. Therefore, the family enjoys a pleasant, comfortable, godly atmosphere.

3. He does his utmost to draw his family to God. He leads the way in right relationships, first to God, then to others. He shows the family, by example, the way of confession, repentance, and restitution, for God's sake.

4. There are times when his wife faces severe trials and is tempted in anguish and calamities, yet her leader points her to God and what is best for her spiritual well-being. Joys and sorrows are mutually shared.

5. Even in the midst of a hostile world, the family enjoys the sweet table of fellowship and devotion to God and to each other. Even as olive oil has many different uses, so the wife

encourages her leader in many ways to fulfill his important position of headship. Therefore, she is blessed, and the blessings cannot all be contained, but overflow to all those around her.

6. God blesses so abundantly . . . there are beautiful and good things to enjoy; pleasant, favorable, and lovely things are all around. Blessings are abounding in spiritual life as well as in the everyday life. These are all here for the family to enjoy all the days of their lives. Best of all is to know that this is only a foretaste of their heavenly and eternal home!

---

1. Ervin Hershberger is a longtime Mennonite church leader, Bible teacher and writer. He resides in Somerset County, Pennsylvania.

Goals for a Discreet Life

Say no unkind word about anyone. Be gracious to family and friends alike. Glorify God by speech and way of life. Keep the work done promptly. Keep a mental list of tasks to do in the future . . . so God's Word is not dishonored.

(A free translation of Titus 2:5)

Now

If you have hard work to do,
        Do it now.
Today the skies are clear and blue,
Tomorrow clouds may come in view,
Yesterday is not for you;
        Do it now.

If you have a song to sing,
        Sing it now.
Let the notes of gladness ring
Clear as song of bird in Spring.
Let every day some music bring;
        Sing it now.

If you have kind words to say,
        Say them now.
Tomorrow may not come your way.
Do a kindness while you may,
Loved ones will not always stay;
        Say them now.

If you have a smile to show,
        Show it now.
Make hearts happy, roses grow,
Let the friends around you know
The love you have before they go;
        Show it now.

—Anonymous

Courtesy of Sword of the Lord Publishers, Murfreesboro, TN, 1969.
Used by permission.

9

Home—Order or Disorder?

"Work well planned is work half done" is a slogan I have learned to appreciate. More recently though, this quote has become alive: "I plan my work, but I work God's plan." I can plan my work with the stipulation that God is in control. Since He views "the whole," my plans are always subject to change.

Order in the home makes it possible to enjoy living even though we think the day is already fuller than can be contained. There is a calm assurance that the blessings come by working God's plan. Flexibility is a prerequisite for planning in an orderly way and then working God's plan. Working God's plan not only brings an orderly, uncluttered mind; it also brings a submissive heart.

I believe organizing is the only way to bring stability into the home. There is freedom in orderliness, and it is a virtue we so desperately need in a world of confusion and disarray. At times we may feel bound to disorder and cluttered living. As husbands and wives, we are to help and encourage each other to become more organized. Organization brings release from the pressures of life.

According to Webster, *organization* or *order* is "a process of arranging so the whole works as a unit with each element having a proper function." First, it is a process, which means it is always ongoing. We never complete organization. I like to think of "the whole" as the family. There are many functions in the home, yet the chief purpose in all areas is to bring glory to God.

So, for our homes to function properly, all elements must function properly. There needs to be a continual process of fitting life together to have a pleasant and God-centered atmosphere.

To be organized, we need a schedule. At times "no" is the best reply to requests that conflict with the schedule we feel God would have us establish. Scheduling brings relaxation because it defeats frenzy and hurry. Order and flexibility bring freedom to begin new tasks or stop old ones without confusion and guilt. Because time has been taken to arrange, organize, and schedule without feeling guilty or fearful, we are permitted calmly to switch tasks as situations change.

Goals are a must in an orderly home. Goals can be described as tasks that need to be completed. They should be achievable. At times they must be broken into subgoals or objectives, thereby making them attainable.

"Let all things be done decently and in order" (1 Corinthians 14:40). Since God is a God of order, this virtue will also characterize His children.

An orderly home is needed in this disorderly society. It is imperative to arrange family priorities. God's will must have priority in all that occurs. With God as the center, all other interests will be brought into line to bring glory to Him.

Essential in arranging priorities and order is good communication. There must be time allotted so every member can express the feelings of his heart in an atmosphere that is relaxed and caring. Parents must plan time for this all-important growing factor in the orderly home. Parents must first be convinced that order is needed so the home can function properly. Only then can children be taught and trained to love and appreciate an orderly, well-arranged family unit. Children will not learn order on their own; they must be trained to appreciate an orderly environment. *"In thee, O LORD, do I put my trust: let me never be put to confusion"* (Psalm 71:1).

Consistency is another valuable ingredient in the orderly home. It is so important to consider prayerfully any issue that arises, then make the decision and stay with the conclusion consistently and humbly. To view any situation from God's perspective, we must have His wisdom, the knowledge of His Word, and an understanding of what God's will is.[1] Punctuality not only includes being on time, but promptness in meeting every requirement during the day. This requires self-denial and the discipline to resist the temptation to waste time, with a willingness to sacrifice ease of pleasure for the sake of future and present well-being.

Cooperation also is needed. This comes as a result of confidence. Parents must seek for every possible occasion to foster and strengthen cooperation in the home.

The virtue of neatness, including cleanliness, is a personal duty in every orderly home. This includes not only personal cleanliness, but also neatness in everything that is possessed, used, or done. Accuracy in word, work, and conduct is a virtue essential for order. People must be trained to see, hear, think, remember, speak, write, and perform all duties with accuracy.

The virtue of quietness includes control of one's natural conduct and impulse to talk. It is possible that more spiritual progress can be made in moments of silence, in the awesome presence of God, than in hours of talking. Quietness makes continuous and fruitful thinking possible. The virtue of industry involves the steady putting forth of energy. This development calls for many choices. Especially in the home, there are constant demands to keep the seemingly insignificant duties up-to-date. Industry is the discipline that prepares one to *"endure hardness."*[2] Industry does not always bring quick rewards, but Ecclesiastes 9:10 reminds us to do with our might what our hands find to do.

Prompt obedience is the only obedience that God accepts. Slow obedience is no obedience at all; therefore, it is imperative to obey promptly. Truthfulness is very essential. To lack truthfulness is to experience more than defeat—it spells disaster! Truth must ring loud and clear. Motivation is important to achieve proper goals. High and worthy motives build strong and noble character.

Proverbs 24:3, 4 gives us the blueprint for an orderly home.

Through wisdom is an house builded; and by understanding it is established: And by knowledge shall the [rooms] *be filled with all precious and pleasant riches.*

Yes, it is possible to have an orderly home in a disorderly world by planning our work, then working God's plan.

---

1. Ephesians 5:17.
2. 2 Timothy 2:3.

Success

Before God's throne to confess
I knelt and bowed my head.
"I failed," I wailed. The Master said,
"Thou didst thy best—that is success."

Parent's Prayer

O heavenly Father, make me a better parent. Teach me to understand my children, to listen patiently to what they have to say, and to answer all their questions kindly. Keep me from interrupting them or contradicting them. Make me as courteous to them as I would have them be to me. Forbid that I should ever laugh at their mistakes, or resort to shame or ridicule when they displease me. May I never punish them for my own selfish satisfaction or to show my power. Let me not tempt my children to lie or steal. And guide me hour by hour that I may demonstrate by all I say and do that honesty produces happiness. Reduce, I pray, the meanness in me. And when I am out of sorts, help me, O Lord, to hold my tongue. May I ever be mindful that my children are children, and I should not expect of them the judgment of adults. Let me not rob them of the opportunity to wait on themselves and to make decisions. Bless me with the bigness to grant them all their reasonable requests and the courage to deny them privileges I know will do them harm. Make me fair and just and kind. And fit me, O Lord, to be loved and respected and imitated by my children.

Courtesy of Baxter Lane Company, Amarillo, TX, 1975.
Used by permission.

10

Children—Strength or STRESS?

*T*here are many similarities between teaching our children and the art of gardening. Three basics are needed in both: a vision, a method, and the finished product.

Early in spring, gardeners browse through seed catalogs and check for better techniques. So also in the life of a young couple, it is with great anticipation that they shop, plan, and prepare for their new baby. Both have a vision of a perfect plan. What a blessing it is to prepare the garden spot, sow the seed, ask God's blessing, and watch the seedlings come through the soft earth as the warm sun and gentle showers keep the ground in perfect condition for growth. If gardeners stopped here, it would not be long until the weeds would take over and choke out the seedlings.

What a blessing a little baby is—pure, innocent, and "angelic"—but not for long! Babies show their human nature as they want what they want now, with no consideration for their parents. Wise parents hold their babies tightly when they stiffen to show their self-will. Parents gently and consistently instill in them what the word "no" means.

And thou shalt teach them diligently unto thy children,
and shalt talk of them when thou sittest in thine house,
and when thou walkest by the way, and when thou liest
down, and when thou risest up (Deuteronomy 6:7).

We must shape our children's behavior early. This takes
place by constant teaching: when walking or traveling, when
eating or reading to the children, or when working. (Little
children should play where the mother works so they can
communicate.) "Every child is capable of being obedient," says
Brother John Risser.[1] "We may excuse low grades in academics,
but there is no excuse for misbehavior."

In Judges 13:1-14, we read the interesting account of the
angel's visit with Manoah and his wife. Manoah asked the
angel a challenging question that each parent should ask God:
"How shall we order the child?" The angel told them to do all
that God commands. In Deuteronomy 6:5, 6 we find God's
command:

And thou [parents] *shalt love the* LORD *thy God with*
all thine heart, and with all thy soul, and with all thy
might . . . these words . . . shall be in thine heart.

Only then are we able to teach our children. Just as the
angel gave Manoah and his wife some practical instruction, so
God also has given us some precise instructions that must be
followed. God has promised wisdom to carry out His plan.

None of us lacks a goal or vision for what we desire, be it
for our children or for our garden. Few are willing to pay the
price for proper priorities, or to change goals in order to get the
desired results of godly children who will be a strength to our
homes, the church, and the community. There is a tendency
to be too involved in the material pursuits of life and not to
spend proper time to nurture and train our children.

Psalm 112:1-5 describes the godly home: *"Blessed* [fully satisfied] *is the man* [home] *that feareth the* L ORD, *that delighteth greatly in his commandments."* Children from such homes will be *"mighty upon* [the] *earth."* Mighty children are not mediocre. They strengthen and uphold the statutes of the Lord; therefore, *"the generation of the upright shall be blessed."* Verses 3 to 5 mention that a godly person will have a proper concept of wealth and riches. Righteousness shall be his first concern. He will be one who is generous, gracious, and full of compassion because he guides all his affairs with godly discretion.

In a home such as this, parents are able to require prompt obedience from their children, a ready response when called, an answer when spoken to, obedience and following through with instruction. Since parents teach more by their attitudes and their way of life, it is very important that they live what they teach.

A garden left to itself does not remain weed-free. The lives of children must also be tended with diligence. It is much easier to keep the garden looking clean and productive when tiny weeds are taken care of systematically and promptly. The same is true with children. It is much better to teach and "nip the bud" of sin than to allow misbehavior to become uncontrollable.

A disrespectful first grader was reprimanded several times by his teacher. When his mother was informed, she explained that such behavior is not acceptable. He was required to apologize. When his mother asked him what his teacher said when he apologized, he said she didn't say anything. It was obvious that the child had not taken the proper steps. Mother then told her son that now he had two violations against him. She took him to his teacher's home and he apologized personally. Punishment was needed because he disobeyed his parents. It is imperative to follow through with consistent discipline. What God has designed to be the strength of the family, Satan uses to undermine.

Children, as well as gardens, need discipline. Amos 3:2 says, *"You only have I known of all the families of the earth: therefore I will punish you for all your iniquities."* The family is still special to God. For its best, God has planned a unique order: father, mother, and children. God expects discipline in the family unit. Discipline produces respect for the home as God's perfect plan, which in return results in respect for God and others.

Acknowledging God as supreme is vital in training children. *"Except the LORD build the house, they labour in vain that build it"* (Psalm 127:1a). God is not building our home unless we communicate and really get through to our children by challenging and arousing their minds to see the truth and then to make the truth their own. By obeying and loving God and the family, we are authentically living in the fear of the Lord and living by His commandments on a daily basis.

Amram and Jochebed were good examples of instilling conviction in the heart and life of young Moses. Years later, his decisions affected the children of Israel. Because of his parents' teaching, he chose to suffer affliction with God's children rather than to enjoy the pleasures of sin for a season because he looked on the reward.[2] Moses not only had a vision, he also had a method to fulfill God's plan because his goal was to follow God's will. No wonder God gave testimony of Moses *"whom the LORD knew face to face"* (Deuteronomy 34:10b).

Psalm 144:12 gives a reason for parents to be good examples to their children:

> *That our sons may be as plants grown up in their youth;*
> *that our daughters may be as corner stones, polished*

after the similitude of a palace."

Certainly we could say, "*Blessed* [happy] *is the nation* [family] *whose God is the* LORD" (Psalm 33:12a).

The stronger the foundation of the home, the greater will be the strength of the children, and the more generations following will be blessed. Sons grown up and daughters as polished cornerstones are the finished products! These qualities are the stability and the strength that is needed in generations to come.

Yes, there are many similarities between nurturing children and gardening. Much effort is needed, as well as lots of patience and hard work. But if neglected, both will bring STRESS.

I composed the following list of guidelines for parents of teenagers.

Do's and Don'ts for Parents of Teenagers Who Desire Their Children to Be a Strength!

1. Don't fly off the handle. Stay calm; children need to know how much better things turn out when parents are self-controlled.

2. Don't depend on vacations and luxuries as a crutch when things get rough. Children are real imitators.

3. Do be strict; show who is in authority. Youth need to know that parents give strong support. When parents "cave in," teenagers get scared.

4. Do act your age. Don't dress or try to talk like a teenager. It is embarrassing, and it looks ridiculous.

5. Do show by your life and conduct that God is in control. Teenagers need to believe in One greater and stronger than their problems.

6. Don't allow them to lie, steal, or be cruel. Be hard on them. Explain why what they do is wrong! Impress upon them

the importance of not repeating such behavior.

7. Don't allow them to go unpunished; administer it. But let them know you still love them even though they let you down. It will make them think twice before they do the same thing again.

8. Don't compromise! Make clear what you mean and mean what you say. Stand up to them and they will respect you; they really don't want everything they ask for.

9. Be honest. Tell them the truth, no matter what, and be straight about everything. They can take it. Lukewarm and shady answers make them uneasy and insecure.

10. Do praise them when they deserve it, and they will be able to handle criticism much easier.

---

1. John Risser is a longtime Mennonite Church leader, evangelist, and Bible teacher. He resides in Rockingham County, Virginia.
2. Hebrews 11:24-26.

*Be such a woman, and live such a life
that if every woman were such as you,
and every life like yours,
this earth would be God's paradise.*

He Leadeth Me

In pastures green? Not always!
Sometimes He who knoweth best, in kindness leadeth me
In many ways where heavy shadows be out of the sunshine,
Warm and soft and bright.
Out of the sunshine, into the darkest of night.
I oft would faint with sorrow and of fright,
Only for this—I know He holds my hand.
So whether in the green or desert land
I trust, although I may not understand.

—Author unknown.

11

The Reflex of Obedience

$\mathcal{T}$ he story is told of a young son of a missionary couple in Brazil who was playing under a tree in their yard. Suddenly, the voice of the boy's father rang out clearly and commandingly, "Philip, obey me instantly! Drop to your stomach!" Immediately the youngster did as he was told. "Now crawl toward me as fast as you can!" The boy obeyed. "Stand up and run to the house." Philip responded unquestioningly and ran to his father. As the youngster turned to look back at the tree, he saw a large poisonous snake hanging from a branch, right above where he had been playing. Because of his "reflex of obedience," his life had been spared. Philip could have hesitated and asked, "Why?" or he could have casually replied, "Wait a minute." But it was his prompt obedience that proved a blessing.

Reflex, according to Webster, is "the power of acting or responding with unique speed; an habitual and predictable way of thinking or behaving."

Luke 5:4-9 gives an interesting account of obedience. The disciples had fished all night and caught nothing. The next morning Jesus told them, *"Launch out into the deep, and let down your nets for a draught."* Peter, seemingly, was the spokesman, and he informed Jesus about the previous night. *"Master, we have toiled all the night and have taken nothing."*

Yet he said, *"Nevertheless at thy word I will let down the net."*
What a wonderful example of the "reflex of obedience"! Like
Peter, we may feel we know best because we have experienced
a certain defeat. Nevertheless, because God's Word is truth,[1] it
is forever settled in heaven. Therefore, it behooves us to obey
the truth promptly.

In 1 Samuel 15, we have an account that is striking in its
lack of the "reflex of obedience." Saul made excuses for his
disobedience, then later blamed the people. As a result, he
discovered that God means what He says and that excuses do
not stand. Through disobedience, he lost God's blessings, his
kingdom, and later his own life. The prophet Samuel reminded
Saul that *"to obey is better than sacrifice."* Never will sacrifice
suffice when God's Word is to be obeyed.

Peter experienced God's blessings by habitual and predictable behavior. In contrast, Saul failed by taking his own way,
not waiting for Samuel, taking things into his own hands,
making excuses, and finally blaming the people for becoming
impatient.

When God speaks to us about a matter, our obedience
must be prompt and unquestioning. When we respond with
prompt, unquestioning obedience, we show the genuineness
of our faith in God's Word and the reality of our love for the
Lord. "True faith obeys while doubt delays" is a slogan that we
must keep in mind. Since Christ dwells in our hearts by faith,
we will be *"rooted and grounded in love."* Only then are we able
to comprehend the breadth, length, depth, and height and to
know the love of Christ, which passes knowledge, being filled
with all the fullness of God (Ephesians 3:17-19).

God told Joshua:

Only be thou strong and very courageous, that thou

*mayest observe to do according to all the law . . . turn
not from it to the right hand or to the left, that thou
mayest prosper* [do wisely] *whithersoever thou goest*
(Joshua 1:7).

Since obedience is the foundation in God's Word, it is
vitally important. *"If the foundations be destroyed, what can
the righteous do?"* (Psalm 11:3). When we view obedience as
the foundation of God's will, we count it a privilege to obey
willingly. Those obeying God are on the winning side now and
eternally. As parents, what is our reflex of obedience? We may
well expect immediate obedience from our children, but does
our heavenly Father receive such obedience from us? Obedience should not be viewed as a "have to," but as something to
be done willingly and joyously by God's grace. What a joy to
serve, love, and obey God faithfully each day of our life.

When I learn to give up my will for God's will, God will
bless me with the same measure of His power to live obediently
and joyously. Therefore, when we surrender in full obedience,
we will be blessed by faith in God in the same proportion.

Malachi 3:6a says, *"For I am the LORD, I change not."* What
a security to know that our heavenly Father does not change!
He speaks once; that is sufficient. He always leads and convicts
through His Word, but He never blindly condemns. God gave
us His Holy Spirit, His holy Word, and His holy Son. He made
every provision for our spiritual welfare. But the choice is up
to us whether we will heed or not. When we really love God,
we will want to know Him and His will. Then our response
will be obedience—cheerful, willing, loving obedience. That
is the kind of reflex God is seeking.

---

1. John 17:17.

Teach Me

Teach me, O Lord, to be sweet and gentle
  In all events of life; in
Disappointments, in the thoughtlessness
  Of others, in the insincerity of those
I trusted, in the unfaithfulness of those
  On whom I relied. Teach me to profit by
The suffering that comes across my path.
  May no one be less good for having
Come within my influence; no one less
  Pure, less true, less kind, less noble for
Having been a fellow-traveler in our
  Journey toward eternal life.

Courtesy of Baxter Lane Company, Amarillo, TX, 1975.
Used by permission.

12

Yoked or Tied?

*A*s a child growing up with horse and buggy, I remember my parents taking a special interest in good quality horses. Several times they bought one that no longer qualified for the racetrack, yet was still a good, high-spirited horse. Since these horses were registered and had good pedigrees, we raised colts for a number of years. What excitement these little, wobbly, "all-legs" creatures brought! But their freedom was short-lived. Mom believed that early, strict discipline would make a good, dependable horse, just as she believed in strict discipline for her own offspring.

At only a few weeks old, a halter was put on the colt. Poor thing! It would shake its head, buck, and kick. Mom stayed nearby to make sure no injuries occurred. Over and over again, the halter was put on the colt. Next, the colt was tied with a rope. The colt again kicked, bucked, and tore around until it was completely worn out. All the while, Mom was standing nearby, talking and trying to calm the unruly animal. Again and again the procedure would be repeated, and again and again the colt would resist when pressure was put on its freedom. Because Mom was a strong woman, she did not give up, but looked beyond the discomforts of the present, envisioning a good, dependable horse for years to come.

How much like an unbroken colt is the person who allows the circumstances of life to govern his moods! One day he is on cloud nine, and the next he is on rock bottom. One day he is joking and laughing, and the next he is depressed and striking out at some innocent person.

Our spiritual maturity is often measured by the way we respond to our circumstances when things go wrong. Do we become depressed and blame others, or do we see God in every situation and allow His grace and strength to carry us through the trying time? Our attitudes toward difficulties reveal whether we have Christ within or merely profess to have Him. When self-will, self-effort, and self-life end at Calvary, then we will be able to see God in everything. Because our hearts have been made pure by His blood, we no longer cater to self, but instead, *". . . I die daily"* (1 Corinthians 15:31).

While traveling in Latin America some time ago, we noted with interest their oxen and cart mode of transportation. It was a beautiful scene to see the two oxen yoked together, walking in unison, sharing the same load, having the same goal. Then another scene comes to mind of another team. One was a mature ox, plodding in sure, steady steps, but beside him was a younger one, resisting, balking, pushing, and shoving. Blisters rubbed on his neck and horns. It was obvious this one was tied, not yoked.

Many times we waste God's precious time by resisting and resenting rather than willingly accepting Jesus' yoke and learning from Him.

> *Come unto me, all ye that labour and are heavy laden, and I will give you rest. Take my yoke upon you, and learn of me. . . . For my yoke is easy, and my burden is light* (Matthew 11:28-30).

Just as resistance and resentment to authority is punished in our homes, so it is also in God's perspective. God often needs to press the point hard until we learn to give Him our first priority.

Often we could have a much more joyful and blessed life if only we would learn from Jesus and walk lovingly and obediently, because we love our heavenly Father and we love to do His will.

O Lord, give me a joyful heart,
One that is tried and true;
So that when troubles and trials are my lot,
I'll still be loving and praising You.

JESUS AND I

I cannot make it alone
The waves dash fast and high;
The fog comes chilling around
And the light goes out in the sky.
But I know that, we too, shall win in the end,
Jesus and I.

Coward and wayward and weak
I change with the changing sky.
Today so strong and brave,
Tomorrow too weak to fly.
But—He never gives in, so we two, shall win,
Jesus and I.

—Author unknown

Life's Challenge

The way is long and often steep;
*   No easy path we find*
To make our lives both strong and deep,
*   A blessing to mankind.*
Through difficulties to the stars,
*   Be this our purpose high,*
And loyal, valiant soldiers be
*   Whether we live or die.*

All those who lean on idle oars,
*   Content to drift along,*
Will never know life's highest joys
*   Nor sing the victor's song.*
Through difficulties to the stars
*   May this our watchword be.*
For those who shun the battle scars,
*   There is no victory.*

Great oaks from little acorns grow
*   But not in one short year.*
Through summer's heat and winter's cold
*   They neither shrink nor fear.*
And so may we in life's hard test
*   Press onward to the goal.*
Devote our talents to the best
*   In body, mind, and soul.*

—Author unknown

13

Noticed or Noble?

*O*n several occasions, young mothers have mentioned their adjustments when they changed careers. Their earlier jobs often included teaching school, secretarial work, or other vocations that called for them to be noticed. One mentioned that homemaking was like stepping from the bright sunlight to the dim shadows. Although the calling of a homemaker is quiet and hidden, it is, nevertheless, a noble calling.

It is important as mothers and homemakers that we learn "to possess outstanding qualities amid a society that would rather be noticed than be willing to do the unnoticed things of life." God chooses ordinary women to do noble work. Faithfulness to God, even though it is done in ordinary, unnoticed tasks, honors God. In John 15:16 we find the phrase *"I have chosen you."* This should challenge us to gladly let God have His way. We must be willing to do the noble work of homemaking rather than preferring a work that is more noticed.

Our life must be characterized by the fruit of the Spirit. Love, joy, and peace need to be our way of life. Longsuffering, gentleness, and goodness pertain to the way we work with our families and people in general. Faithfulness, meekness, and temperance refer to our inward character. With these, we are equipped to better fulfill that noble work to which God calls us because we have availed ourselves of the grace of God for the task that needs to be accomplished. *"But to every one of us is given grace according to the measure of the gift of Christ"* (Ephesians 4:7). We must always remember, "I cannot, but God can!"

The woman of Shunem, described in 2 Kings 4:8-17, is a prime example of a noble woman. She was not necessarily noticed by her peers, but she filled her place well in her home. Because she was a noble woman of outstanding qualities, she was not content only to care for her husband, but rather her compassion reached out to others. She had the courage to meet the needs of the man of God who passed that way often and needed a place to rest.

Elisha was so impressed by her actions that he wanted to show her kindness. He asked her what she would desire: *"What is to be done for thee? wouldest thou be spoken for to the king, or to the captain of the host?"* Her answer is another reason why she is considered a noble woman: *"And she answered, I dwell among mine own people."* Such a quality is rare indeed! That is the virtue of contentment. She had no need, because she found herself as she freely gave to meet the needs of her friends and those in need.

A noble man by the name of Gutenberg invented the printing press in 1460. It wasn't until years later that Gutenberg stated the reason for his success. In a large dictionary he explained that his work had been done under "the protection of the All-Highest who often reveals to the humble what He conceals from the wise." Very little is known about Gutenberg. Not a single portrait was made of him during his lifetime. No one has discovered even one line of his handwriting. We do know, however, that Gutenberg's printing press made it possible for new ideas to be published and spread. Most of all, his efforts were most keenly felt in Christianity, all because he was willing to do a noble work without recognition.

Nobility does not have to be in the forefront, doing only the great and awesome jobs. Nobility is evident in the character of a meek and quiet spirit that willingly toils even though the deeds go unnoticed.

In Mark 12:41-44 we read the account of the poor widow who humbly placed two mites (which would be less than a penny) into the treasury. As always, Jesus was observing! Jesus also noticed that some gave much and allowed their giving to be seen, while this poor widow gave *"all that she had, even all her living."*

The scribes are an example of people who loved to be noticed for their much giving, their much praying, and their pious living. Yet Jesus was not impressed. He pointed out that they already had all the reward they were going to get.[1]

Recently, we were confronted with a decision. A phone call informed us of the drowning of a young relative, hundreds of miles away. We made an attempt to attend the funeral. Because of the distance, aircraft was the only possible way of travel, but the rates were very high. After talking about the incident, we decided that even though we could not be there for the funeral, there are other ways that comfort and encouragement could be given. We could make a phone call to share our sympathy with the sorrowing family. We could also let them know our concern by taking time to write and send a sympathy card. This could be read and reread. But somehow what *I* really wanted to do was attend the funeral rather than be content to do the seemingly little, unnoticed deed. To us, the task may seem small and insignificant, but to God it is His character that shines forth if we are willing to be used and give all the glory to Him.

The noble woman or man remembers yesterday with joy, lives today with enthusiasm, and looks forward to tomorrow with confidence knowing it is God who is being served, and that it is God therefore who will notice and reward noble deeds.

---

1. Matthew 6:5.

*God has two dwellings—one in heaven,
the other in a meek and thankful heart.*

Marriage Takes Three

I once thought marriage took
Just two to make a go.
But now I am convinced
It takes the Lord also.

And not one marriage fails
Where Christ is asked to enter,
As lovers come together
With Jesus at the center.

But marriage seldom thrives
And homes are incomplete
Until He's welcome there
To help avoid defeat.

In homes where Christ is first,
It's obvious to see,
Those unions really work,
For marriage still takes three.

Perry Tanksley, ©1990.
Used by permission.

14

God's Hedge of Protection

*I*t is evident that marriage relationships are deteriorating; therefore, homes are breaking down in our society. Satan is very busy trying to destroy, but with God's help, marriages can be preserved. God can provide the inner force to hold a marriage together. Just as God physically holds the atoms in our body together, He is available to be the unseen strength in the marital union. God is willing to establish and perfect a marriage where He is acknowledged as Lord because He loves His people and has a purpose in mind. God has promised that *"a threefold cord is not quickly broken"* (Ecclesiastes 4:12b).

It is interesting to note the guidelines God gave to Adam and Eve.

> *Therefore shall a man leave his father and his mother, and shall cleave unto his wife: and they shall be one flesh. And they were both naked . . . and were not ashamed* (Genesis 2:24, 25).

Adam did not have parents to instruct him with marriage guidelines. He and Eve were not tempted to infidelity because they were the only human beings created. But God gave them the blueprint for their relationship in the first portion of His

Word, right at the creation, before any transgressions or questions.

So also today, we must have guidelines and rules early in marriage that are based on God's holy Word in order for us to be faithful to God and to each other. Are we fully aware of God's wonderful love for us? Even in the twenty-first century, God's Word is still the whole truth. It has not and will not change. God is still the third person in marriage.

In Genesis 2:24, 25, the word *"leave"* commands the husband to depart from his parents and all others and *"cleave"* to his wife. The husband and wife are commanded to cleave like two pieces of wood glued together, so close that not even the wedge of unkindness or disloyalty can get between them. Romans 8:31 tells us that *"if God be for us, who can be against us?"* This can be paraphrased for husband and wife: "If husband and wife are for each other, even Satan cannot be against them, because God is that inner force that holds them together."

Only then can they experience the unity that God desires, that of "becoming one flesh." They will be one in their individual love for God, one in church matters, one in understanding God's Word and His will, and one in following His way. They will be one in life's vocation, one in material and financial pursuits, and one in building their home and training their children. Yes, they will be united because God is their eternal God; they will be one in seeking, trusting, and acknowledging God in everything. God does not demand that the couple think alike, but that they think together.

Mary Pride, in her book *The Way Home*, describes the difference between a biblical and an intimate marriage. In the biblical marriage, romance is the flower of marriage, not the root. The intimate marriage consists of thrills and excitement; therefore, it is self-centered rather than God-centered. God is the root, that inner force, that blesses the unity of a couple with a physical and romantic love that pleases Him. This is possible only as God is included and His blueprint carefully followed.

Yes! God has an hedge about the faithful family. Job's family is a good example of one that experienced God's blessing. That is why Satan accused God, *"Hast not thou made an hedge about him, . . . and about all that he hath on every side?"* (Job 1:10).

God's hedges are not necessarily protections from trials. In Job's experience, God's hedge did not keep Satan from afflicting Job. Rather, God's hedge of protection kept Job from cursing God or just giving up. Every trial or affliction that comes into our lives has first passed God's approval. God sees it for our best, but Satan desires only to accuse God and bring disgrace to Him.

In our marriage, God has not always given us an easy life. Bennie and I both were widow's children. His mother lived with us the first five years of our marriage and that added pressure. During our years of young parenting, we experienced several hospital stays with our two oldest children. After we had been married 17 years, Bennie suddenly became sick and had emergency surgery in Columbus, Ohio, where he was involved in church work. Three months later he had corrective surgery. The same year I also had two major surgeries. Down through the years, we have had occasional financial setbacks. We also have experienced some unpleasant relationships in church life, but in it all, God's hedge of protection has been the factor that kept us pressing closer to God. Yes, there were times when we failed and became discouraged. But the trials we faced drew us closer together as husband and wife and closer to our heavenly Father, the One we knew had planned that we share the joys and sorrows of life together, and the

One who knows what is best for us.

Marriages are made and recognized in heaven, but husbands and wives must maintain their marriages. God gave the foundation and the families, but it is up to us to abide within that hedge of protection. Marriage is meant to be a blessed relationship, but it is up to each couple whether it will be a blessing or a strain.

Since God's Word is truth, any slight deviation is to move from the truth. For any individual, husband, wife, or parent, there is a narrow road called truth for all to follow closely. To choose that path and remain on it is to follow God's direction. When we decide to no longer meet all of God's requirements, we are choosing to leave the path of truth and the hedge of God's protection.

Ephesians 5 gives us some very timely advice. The first step is to follow God as dear children, walking in obedience. We are to love God with all our heart and to live the sacrificial life of Christ. We must confess and forsake all sin. We are to live a life of thanksgiving and praise to God by living the fruit of the Spirit: goodness, righteousness, and truth. This is the only way to walk circumspectly, as wise people, being careful to use time carefully and wisely.

When God fills the couple, there is no room for selfish pursuits or worldly excitement. Instead, they are quiet and live a contented, godly life in God's will. By following God's pattern, it is easy and blessed to submit to one another as husband and wife, in submission to Christ, the Head. Therefore, the husband loves his wife and children with the same sacrificial love Christ showed for the church, always desiring and striving for their spiritual well-being.

Job is an outstanding example of one who had a sacrificial

love for his family. He offered sacrifices and prayers just in case his family sinned.[1] No wonder Satan was jealous and envious of all the glory God was receiving! Satan still cannot stand to see a God-fearing family; therefore, he is trying to destroy it yet today. But we need not despair because that same hedge[2] is still available for every couple. Every fiery dart of Satan must first pass God's approval before it dare touch us. We can, by God's grace, be protected as we follow God's formula carefully.

In school I learned a rule that is still wise to follow:

Good, better, best
Never let it rest
Until the good is better,
And the better is best!

In marriage, this should be the rule: a constant desire to mature and grow in God's likeness, not being satisfied, but continually growing in holiness. We dare not desire to live "the springtime of our marriage in the shadows of autumn." Rather, we must enjoy each stage of life, recognizing God's blessings, always pressing toward higher plains of spiritual perfection. As *"iron sharpeneth iron,"*[3] so must we polish and encourage each other to become more godly.

We dare not compare our marriage with other marriages. We are reminded in 2 Corinthians 10:12 not to compare ourselves among ourselves, for this is not wise, although we should learn and grow from the experiences of others. Covetousness and sinful fantasizing does not belong to the Christian marriage. Someone has suggested that most marriage problems are spiritual problems that are compounded when a couple marries. God is left out; therefore, the two pursue their own selfish desires. The answer is not merely to pray more and read the Bible more, or just to go from here and do better. Rather, the answer is to be crucified with Christ.[4] Dying to self and living unto God represent the only option that brings joy and peace, allowing Christ total control of our lives.

Our baptismal and marriage vows both included a commitment to God, in which we said "no" to the world and our selfish desires and "yes" to living for God for the rest of our lives. God holds us accountable for such a commitment. He demands total dedication! Commitment brings communication, and communication brings confidence. It is sad that confidence is seemingly a word of the past.

Husband and wife can be likened to a lock and key. Together they accomplish their purpose, but apart they are of little value. In their proper role, they are equally important because they complement and complete each other.

When couples seek God,[5] they experience a security because the whole family knows that the central point is always God. There is no confusion because God is loved with all the heart and all the soul and all the mind (Matthew 22:37).

At times we take our spouse or children for granted. We think they should know what we mean, when we really never communicated.

Flattery, flirtation, and suggestive jesting are sins to which we dare not yield. Beware of the power of the tongue! *"Death and life are in the power of the tongue"* (Proverbs 18:21a). *"For out of the abundance of the heart the mouth speaketh"* (Matthew 12:34b). *"Whoso keepeth his mouth and his tongue keepeth his soul from troubles"* (Proverbs 21:23). God expects us to be discreet in our speech as well as in our lifestyle. We must be able to hold our peace. *"The discretion of a man deferreth his anger"* (Proverbs 19:11a). The key for controlling our tongue is found in Ephesians 4:15a: *"But speaking the truth in love, [we] may grow up into him in all things....*" God's love in one's heart is defined as the act of one person seeking the highest good in one's spouse, an unselfish concern for the other's spiritual well-being. With an attitude such as this, we will be humble and quick to confess when we have wronged our spouse or family. We must acknowledge our humanity, thereby feeling with them and sharing our desire for them to grow in Christ. Confession is good for the soul!

Consecration to God must be wholehearted. It is in the transformed, consecrated heart that God dwells and Satan is defeated. When we live and walk in the Spirit,[6] it is evident that God's hedge of protection is about us. We cannot claim to be walking in God's Spirit when we become angry and place blame on our spouse. In doing so, we grieve the blessed Holy Spirit. When problems arise—and they will—each obstacle must be confronted with a cool head and a warm heart. God sees the heart and knows who we are rather than who we pretend to be.

God does not give each of us all the gifts of the Spirit, but He does command the Christian to possess all the fruit of the Spirit. When the fruit is absent, we lose our effectiveness in prayer and witness. God expects us to live a holy life because people are looking for examples to follow. Society is observing families, and faithful ones are a powerful witness for God. Since actions speak louder than words, we are judged largely by our actions. Then, if needed, we may use words as an added witness.

"*Being confident of this very thing, that* [God] *which hath begun a good work in you will perform it until the day of Jesus Christ*" (Philippians 1:6). What a blessing to know it is God who is that inner strength, that inner force that holds our marriages together. He has a hedge of protection about the family. Where the blood of Christ is applied, there Christ dwells, and Satan is put to flight.

Yes, God blesses and leads right to the journey's end, and it is He who surrounds us with His hedge of protection along the way.

1. Job 1:5.
2. Job 1:10.
3. Proverbs 27:17.
4. Galatians 2:20.
5. Matthew 6:33.
6. Galatians 5:25.

Bible

B asic
I nformation
B efore
L eaving
E arth

Caring for Each Other

Take care of each other, dear Husband and Wife,
  For time is fleeting, there's no time for strife.
Always be faithful and pray for each other.
  For strong is the power of a praying couple.

Take care of each other, dear Husband and Wife,
  When struggles and trials have entered your life.
For then is the time a faithful companion
  To be to each other must never be ended.

Take care of each other, dear Husband and Wife.
  Consider the ungodly, their house is of strife.
Satan has destroyed it, and maliciously craves
  Your home, your life, and children enslave.

Take care of each other, dear Husband and Wife,
  For Christ in His love for the church gave His life.
He cares for her daily, thru struggles, thru fears.
  For He has once crossed this vale of tears.

Take care of each other, dear Husband and Wife,
  For the night is far spent, eternity is nigh.
Soon comes the cry, the bridegroom is come;
  Then it's too late to do the undone.

—Author unknown

15

Termites in Marriage

What a sense of accomplishment I felt as I straightened my tired back to get a better view of my beautiful, newly waxed hardwood floor. But one thing bothered me. There was a bubble in the floor that I had not noticed before. I mentioned to my husband what I had found. He assured me it was caused by the expansion and contraction of the wood and there was no need to worry. Naturally, I was relieved.

Some months later, I was busy spring-cleaning the living room. As I lifted the oval rug, I discovered not only one bubble but a number of bubbled spots. Again, I showed my husband the floor. This time, he too was concerned. He arranged to have the termite exterminators come and take a look at the floor.

The exterminators determined that termites were indeed present, and they set out to remedy the problem. Six-inch ditches were dug all around the foundation of our house, and holes were drilled on the inside walls of the rooms. The entire house was fumigated. In addition to the high cost, there was lots of hard work, as well as dust and dirt, involved in repairing the damage. After several attempts, the exterminator shared the good news that the infested area was clear of termites.

Statistics show that more structures are destroyed by termites than by fire. Termites cause damage behind the scenes. The very structure may deteriorate before anyone is aware of any damage.

Did you know that marriages also are destroyed by "termites"? Husbands and wives must continually be on guard and sensitive to small, seemingly insignificant areas of their lives.

Perhaps the first "termite" is *"thou hast left thy first love"* (Revelation 2:4b). Someone has said, "If we lose something, we can blame it on someone else, but if we leave an item, the person who left the object is directly responsible to again come back to where he left it." Leaving our first love in marriage is also possible. The agape love, the love that comes from God, is our security against unfaithfulness. It is impossible to have a godly relationship with each other if our relationship with God is not vital and growing. Unless the Bible is closely followed, the secular world and its practices may become the guideline rather than God's holy plan.

Disrespect is another "termite." With the vows we made "before God and these witnesses," we committed our lives to each other "for better or worse, in sickness or health as long as we both shall live." This promise can be taken far too lightly. Just as termites work in darkness, so many marriages imperceptibly deteriorate. We take each other for granted. We fail to appreciate those little tokens and acts of love. Unkind words are uttered, and actions once considered hurtful become the norm. Arguments earlier unthought of are now tolerated. Disrespect becomes the way of life. Courtesy to others outside the family is seemingly more important than courtesy shown to those dearest to us.

Another "termite" that destroys is the absence of a deep spiritual life. A marriage will not likely stand where spiritual values are overlooked. Since God joins two people,[1] it is a spiritual relationship. Conflicts and stresses will not break up a marriage that is held with honor and respect as a sacred gift from God. The spiritual life provides resources for working through difficulties rather than seeking escape.

Selfishness is another "termite." Since man is selfish by nature, self-interest and self-satisfaction are the goal. When two people live together and both live for self, there is bound to be conflict. True godly love motivates a deepening experience in which self dies. Because each is motivated to pursue the joy and security of the other, success in marriage deepens when the emphasis is placed on God. Self-denial takes the place of self-fulfillment.

Immaturity is also a "termite" that causes confusion and chaos. We must seek God's will and have a proper perspective that comes from a pure heart.[2] Then we will not be plagued with the idea that it has to be done our own way, but both will be concerned that it is done in God's way for God's glory. God's way always points to Him, that by *"speaking the truth in love,* [we] *may grow up into him in all things"* (Ephesians 4:15a).

Stubbornness is a "termite" that destroys by hindering God's Spirit from working in submission to each other. Reverence for God and respect for each other are lost when we do not feel the need of help from our spouse. Rather, the attitude is "I'll do it when and how I want to when I feel like it."

Another "termite" that destroys under the surface is covetousness, robbing marriage of contentment, peace, and joy. We tend to have the feeling that contentment is found in things rather than the condition of the heart.

Lack of communication can destroy even the best of marriages. Since there can be no guesswork in the home, husband and wife should say what they mean and mean what they say. (Back to our termite encounter—when Bennie finally realized the seriousness of the matter, his first response was, "Why didn't you mention it sooner?" I had failed in communicating the urgency of the problem.)

Satan knows that materialism is another subtle "termite." When we overobligate ourselves, we become too busy to get all the things done that need our attention. We become irritable and impatient with those dearest to us, and often our spiritual life is neglected. I was once challenged that the spiritual status of a person is gauged by the bookmark in his or her Bible. Does the bookmark move continually, or are we neglecting the most important time of the day? Materialism is usually the cause. To keep our material pursuits in proper order, we need to live by Romans 12:1, 2. Also, we must remember to seek God first. Then *all these things shall be added unto* [us]" (Matthew 6:33b).

The temperaments of husband and wife are usually different. Although this may have drawn the couple together in courtship, frequently these differences can become irritations. Instead, we should allow differences to make us a complete couple. In Judges 13 there is an interesting account of Manoah and his wife. The angel appeared to his wife first. Then Manoah desired also to hear his message. He was called at the angel's second appearance. Their different responses to the angel are interesting. Manoah impulsively responded, *"We shall surely die, because we have seen God."* His wife replied more calmly, *"If the LORD were pleased to kill us, he would not have received a burnt offering and a meat offering at our hands."*

It is God's perfect will that husbands and wives comple-ment each other. At times, we may allow a competitive spirit to prevail, which is another "termite." The root problem is jealousy and envy, even though at times we may not be aware of it. We must certainly plead to God to help us keep our hearts with all diligence.[3] God's plea is for unity and oneness, not disunity and chaos.

The tongue is another "termite" that quickly destroys.

But the tongue can no man tame; it is an unruly evil, full of deadly poison. Therewith bless we God, even the Father; and therewith curse we men, which are made after the similitude of God (James 3:8, 9).

Because of our tongue, it is often too easy to blame others for our wrongs and failures. We cannot bless God and at the same time curse or speak evil of each other.

Many of us do not enjoy changes. Yet we cannot deny the fact that we are growing older and we will need to change in order to continue living. Growing older makes us take a good look at life in the view of eternity. Resistance to change can be a "termite" that destroys. It need not be a burden to grow older. We do well to recognize this. We cannot live in the springtime of marriage as we enter our midlife years. To refuse to acknowledge our age is to refuse to accept God's plan. *"But though our outward man perish, yet the inward man is renewed day by day"* (2 Corinthians 4:16b).

God's plan is always perfect! He knows that if we retained our youthful looks and ambitions, we would fail to see the seriousness of life and the certainty of eternity. In the godly marriage, it is not the physical beauty and zeal that attracts, *"but . . . the hidden man of the heart . . . which is in the sight of God of great price"* (1 Peter 3:4). That is why it is so impor-

tant to build our marriages on the agape love, the only love
that will stand the test of time and be able to exterminate the
"termites."

1. Mark 10:9.
2. Matthew 5:8.
3. Proverbs 4:23.

Anything done without heart
is done in the dark!

God's Will for You and Me

Just to be tender, just to be true
Just to be glad, the whole day through!
Just to be merciful, just to be mild
Just to be trustful, as a child
Just to be gentle and kind and sweet
Just to be helpful with willing feet
Just to be cheery, when things go wrong
Just to drive sadness away with a song.

Whether the hour is dark or bright
Just to be loyal to God and right.
Just to believe, God knows best
Just in His promises ever to rest
Just to let love be our daily key
That is God's will for you and me.

—Author unknown

". . . and serve him with a perfect heart and with a willing mind: for the LORD searcheth all hearts, and understandeth all the imaginations of the thoughts: if thou seek him, he will be found of thee . . ." (1 Chronicles 28:9b).

16

God's Perfect or Permissive Will

"*Set thine house in order; for thou shalt die, and not live*" (2 Kings 20:1b). This was the message the Prophet Isaiah brought to King Hezekiah.

I wonder how a message such as this would affect me. We are all aware that we, too, need continually to set our house in order because we do not know how much time God has allotted to us.

King Hezekiah responded by turning his face to the wall and begging God. He said, "*. . . O LORD, remember now how I walked before thee in truth and with a perfect heart, and have done that which is good in thy sight*" (2 Kings 20:3). Then he wept sore.

God must have changed His mind, because He spoke to Isaiah before he left the court. God sent Isaiah back to King Hezekiah with another message. God said, "*I have heard thy prayer . . . , behold, I will heal thee . . . , I will add unto thy days fifteen years*" (2 Kings 20:5b, 6a). God's perfect will versus His permissive will comes to my mind as I read this account of King Hezekiah.

During the 15 years that God added to the king's life, a
son, Manasseh, was born. He began his reign at the age of 12,
after his father's death. All through 2 Kings 21, we find the evil
deeds of King Manasseh.

More blood was shed during his reign than during any
other king's reign. He built altars to idols and even made his
sons pass through the fire.[1] Much wickedness was the result
of King Hezekiah's desire for God's permissive will rather than
God's perfect will. What is our position? Are we satisfied and
happy with God's perfect will, or do we plead to God and turn
our face to the wall and weep sore?

At his conversion, the Apostle Paul was struck down by a
bright light. His question was, *"Lord, what wilt thou have me
to do?"* (Acts 9:6a). This is the important question. It is still
the result of a person who is seeking God's perfect will. Paul
thought he was doing God's will when he "[breathed] *out
threatenings and slaughter against the disciples of the Lord"*
(Acts 9:1). But when he came face to face with Jesus, he wanted
to know what Jesus' will was for him.

George Mueller's life gives testimony to the perfect will of
God. His simple faith in God was an amazement to the whole
world in his day. Someone once asked him what his formula
was in determining God's divine will, to which he replied, "I
seek at the beginning to get my heart into such a state that it
has no will of its own in regard to a given matter." Most of the
difficulties are overcome when our hearts are ready to do the
Lord's will.

Since Paul was obedient to God in faithfully following
through with God's perfect will, he gives us a blueprint by
which we also are able to find God's perfect will.

I beseech [beg] *you therefore, brethren, by the mercies*

of God, that ye present your bodies a living sacrifice,
holy, acceptable unto God, which is your reasonable
service. And be not conformed to this world: but be ye
transformed by the renewing of your mind, that ye may
prove what is that good, and acceptable, and perfect, will
of God (Romans 12:1, 2).

How wonderful that our heavenly Father gives us precise instructions on how we can find and follow His perfect will!

Step one: "Present your bodies a living sacrifice." This means utter, unreserved, undivided surrender. Often it is in this first step that we fail to follow God's blueprint, and this is why there is so much confusion and unrest in the hearts and lives of Christians today. When I surrender my body as a living sacrifice, it means, *"I am crucified with Christ: nevertheless I live; yet not I, but Christ liveth in me"* (Galatians 2:20a). I claim no rights for myself, but I find in Jesus my all in all.

Step two: "And be not conformed to this world." The world's pattern of life is one of selfishness, sinfulness, materialism, greed, and lust. We are living in a "me first" society. Eyes are blinded to spiritual realities and objectives; therefore, the will of God cannot be perceived. We must pay the price of separation. It costs our whole life and all our motives and actions. We must walk in the light and knowledge of God's Word. Then there will be power to live victoriously, to be well-pleasing to God, and to be approved of men.[2]

Step three: "Be ye transformed by the renewing of your mind." This is only our reasonable service.

Our minds, our spirits, and our entire spiritual lives must constantly be refreshed by dwelling in Christ's presence and feeding on His Word. Unless this is our frame of mind, the perfect will of God cannot be found. A carnally minded person cannot please God.[3]

The whole course of life must be spiritual: a daily, constant walk with God through prayer and reading His Word. This is the only way our lives will be renewed, refreshed, and transformed so that God can bless us with the knowledge of His will.

Why settle for less than God's best? We know that God is pleased when we obediently and joyfully follow Him. With such an attitude, we find joy in fulfilling our tasks. As wives and mothers, we labor long and hard for the sake of God and our families. Those seemingly undesirable tasks become meaningful when we do them as unto the Lord.[4] It is then that we are able to face those hard, unexpected, and frustrating times that are bound to come to all of us. As we daily walk in His presence and live in His fellowship, we will not need to rush to God, asking for a quick answer for an unexpected frustration or emergency. We will find we can experience what the prophet said in Isaiah 30:21: *"Thine ears shall hear a word* [voice] *behind thee, saying, This is the way, walk ye in it, when ye turn to the right hand, and when ye turn to the left."*

---

1. 2 Kings 21:6.
2. Romans 14:18.
3. Romans 8:8.
4. Colossians 3:23.

It is in loving,
*   not in being loved*
The heart finds its quest;
It is in giving,
*   not in getting*
Our lives are blessed.

A Family Prayer

Dear God in heaven, help us to make our home a happy place . . . an orderly home of love, peace, and contentment . . . a place of work and worship . . . where You are always the center and where people known and unknown are always welcome.

Through the passing years, keep us faithful to You and loyal to each other, always keeping within that blessed realm of Your hedge of protection until we reach our eternal home in heaven.

In Jesus' name,
Amen

17

Love Without a "Net"

"Will you love and cherish, in health and in sickness, in prosperity and in adversity, share the joys and sorrows of life, exercising patience, kindness, and forbearance, live in peace as becometh a faithful Christian couple, forsaking all others, keep yourselves only for each other as long as you both shall live?"

Not one of us who has made those vows had any idea what all would be included when we answered, "I will." But we need not worry or be anxious because "[We] *know whom* [we] *have believed and* [are] *persuaded that he* [God] *is able to keep that which* [we] *have committed unto him against that day*" (2 Timothy 1:12b).

When we love without a "net" or stipulation, we free our spouse and our children to become all that God has planned for them to become. For some, this means we must say "yes" to more responsibilities than raising our family or being a supportive church member. To some, this comes early in married life. We must let go and allow God to have our husbands lead the church. Often, God does not wait until we feel we are willing. Neither does God wait until the children are grown. Therefore, it weighs heavily upon the wife to carry added responsibility in teaching and caring for the family in order to free the husband to do God's bidding.

We dare not entertain thoughts such as "I have been neglected" or "my needs are unmet." This would be the first step in squelching our husbands' effectiveness. Attitudes such as these are likened to a net used to catch prized butterflies. All the fluttering is to no avail! But allow the butterfly liberty, and it beautifies the surrounding area. That is how it is in our homes when we allow God to have full control of our husbands' and children's lives. That release blesses and enlarges our capacity to appreciate and enjoy God's vast areas of service, and it brings joy unspeakable and full of glory.[1]

Murmurings and complainings are another "net" that will hinder our effectiveness. At times, I am tempted to think it has been a long time since I had my husband's unhurried attention. Then I recognize that my husband belongs to God first of all. This helps me to find joy and fulfillment in knowing that God comes first. Since *"I am crucified with Christ: nevertheless I live; yet not I, but Christ liveth in me"* (Galatians 2:20a), I will not feel slighted or neglected if God's work takes my husband's or children's time.

If I have no rights of my own, then I have nothing to lose or complain about. Someone has wisely said, "It is much better to have 10 percent of a 100 percent man than to have 100 percent of a 10 percent man." This helps me keep my priorities straight.

Charles Spurgeon is known as one of the greatest eighteenth century evangelists. He was married to Susanna Thompson, a dedicated young woman who was a good example of one who "loved without a net." Charles kept a very busy schedule of speaking engagements around London and throughout the British Isles.

Once when Charles was preparing to leave for another series of meetings, Susanna broke into tears. She did not want him to leave. He had an interesting response: "Susie, do you think when the Israelites brought a lamb as an offering to the Lord they stood and wept over it?" She shook her head, to which he replied, "Well, don't you see that you are giving me to God as your sacrifice in letting me go to preach the Gospel? Do you think God wants you to cry over your sacrifice?"

Perhaps some of us can identify with Susie Spurgeon. But we must be challenged not to weep over what we think is a sacrifice.

It is often true that in marriage opposite temperaments attract each other; this gives much room and many opportunities to grow and to expand our capacities. Charles was known to be a straightforward, uneducated fellow with a "countrified" manner, and his speech often brought more embarrassment than reverence. Susie was just the opposite. She was the daughter of a prosperous merchant. She was proper and reserved, yet it was her dedicated spiritual life that won Charles' heart.

Charles' zeal for God's Word and his burden for God's people coupled with Susie's educated, pious, "proper" Christian life was the combination that God needed to make Charles Spurgeon the outstanding preacher he was.

Susie could have demanded more of Charles' time and attention, but because of her deep devotion to her Lord and Savior, she encouraged her husband to be all that God wanted him to be. She did not confine him to a "net."

The same was true in Charles' life. Since he was uneducated, he was blessed by Susie's ability to read Greek and Hebrew. She often assisted him in his message preparation. Not only was Susie an assistance to Charles' ministry, but she also founded a book fund whereby she distributed thousands of books to others. Many of these were copies of Charles' messages.

Susie was a good mother to their twin boys. Since her husband was a busy man, much of the teaching and training was left for Susie to do. In all this, both of the boys grew up to serve also in the ministry in later years.

Charles not only loved his wife and gave her credit for helping his ministry become successful, but he also encouraged her to find fulfillment in becoming all God wanted her to become.

David Livingston once asked Charles, "How do you manage to do two days' work in a single day?" Charles replied without hesitation, "You forgot there are two of us. My wife and I, we work together."[2] What a challenge! In loving without a "net," much can be accomplished when love comes from a pure heart.[3]

It has been said that fishermen who harvest crabs need never fear losing any crabs once they are netted and placed in a container. They keep each other from escaping! When one begins to climb out of the container, its peers are there to pull it down.

Let it not once be said of us as husbands and wives that our spouse or our children are not free to become all God wants them to become, to rise to levels of maturity, because we are guilty of the "crab treatment."

Loving without a "net" is described as *"putting aside the past, doing our best while living in each day, and earnestly press-*

ing toward the goal of conforming to the image of our Lord and Saviour" (Philippians 3:13, 14, paraphrased).

1. 1 Peter 1:8.
2. William J. Petersen, *Catherine Marshall Had a Husband* (Wheaton, Illinois: Tyndale House Publishers, 1986), pp. 121-156.
3. 1 Timothy 1:5.

Abide in Me

Dear child of my love, why worry and fret
  About things that you must do.
It is "Dying" not "Doing" that bringeth forth fruit,
  And all that I want is "Just YOU."
It's the Life of the tree that flows through the branch,
  That produces the fruit that you see.
And the fruits of the Spirit shall surely be seen
  If you'll just keep "Abiding in Me."

Does the branch ever struggle and try to bear fruit?
  How vain all its efforts would be.
The purpose for which it was formed is attained
  As it stays in its place on the tree.
And the small grain of wheat must fall into the ground
  And die, ere ever new life shall appear.
By its dying, alone comes "Abundance of Life,"
  First the blade, then full corn in the ear.

The beautiful rose and the lily, so fair,
  Never worry or fret; they "just grow."
From whence comes their beauty, their fragrance so sweet
  Only He, who created them, knows.
And to Him who redeemed thee, most precious thou art
  Like a bright shining light, thou shalt be.
With His "Life more Abundant," and such "Fullness of Joy,"
  All thy friends shall see Jesus in thee.

Courtesy of Baxter Lane Company, Amarillo, TX, 1975.
Used by permission.

18

Prepare for the Rainy Day

To many women, rainy days are depressing. But consider the opposite condition—the pressing heat, the dry and brown countryside, the barren and bleak surroundings. We would live in a desert! Rainy days are a blessing from God. How relaxing to watch a gentle rain, to notice black clouds gathering, to hear the welcome sound of thunder, to observe the grandeur of lightning, suddenly to feel the cool, refreshing breeze of an abrupt downpour, and then to discover a beautiful rainbow shortly afterward.

God never forgets His children. Just as He set the rainbow in the clouds as a reminder of His promise never again to destroy the earth by a Flood,[1] so the rainbow is still a sign that God keeps His promises and will never leave nor forsake us.[2] Just as nature needs rain, so we need rainy days to perfect and refresh our spiritual lives. First of all, we need to maintain a vital relationship with our Creator. Our lives must be in order, our sins confessed up-to-date, and encouragement given when there is opportunity. Then, with confidence in God, we can meet the not-so-pleasant experiences in life and acknowledge them as sent from God.

An elderly saint has been a continual inspiration to me. He always has a word of encouragement for everyone. His countenance is always cheerful. When I asked him what his secret is, he replied, "I have never met a disappointment, because years ago I placed a capital *H* where the *d* is in *disappointment*. He further said, "A person can live such a life that as he grows older and looks back, he will have few, if any regrets." He had learned by God's grace to obey God promptly, quickly, and cheerfully.

> *Hear counsel, and receive instruction, that thou mayest be wise in thy latter end. There are many devices in a man's heart; nevertheless the counsel of the LORD, that shall stand* (Proverbs 19:20, 21).

Since thanksgiving and murmuring are not found in the same heart, we must decide how we are going to face life. Either we grumble and complain because self is on the throne and is never satisfied, or we, through thanksgiving and praise, are so busy serving our Master and others that we have no time to lament and complain about that which we don't have.

Guy Doud shares how he prepared for the rainy day. He and his dad had a good father-son relationship, often encouraging each other and sharing hopes and ambitions. After one such memorable evening, they parted, little realizing it was to be their last conversation. Several days later, a phone call alerted Guy that his dad had suffered a massive heart attack. When Guy and his friend entered the embalming room, Joe asked Guy if there was anything he would have liked to tell his dad. With deep respect, Guy said he could think of nothing that he needed to talk to his dad about. "Everything I ever wanted to tell him I did." Their communication was up to date! They both were prepared for the rainy day.[3]

During the 1989 earthquake in San Francisco, California, a certain lady was homeschooling her daughter. The mother gave her daughter the assignments, then hurried to the grocery store. The little girl was tempted to leave her books and play with her cat but decided to obey her mother instead. Suddenly, the earth quaked, crashing the chimney of the house and killing the family cat. What a blessing obedience proved to be! If the daughter had disobeyed, she may have died along with the cat. But through obedience, mother and daughter were both blessed and prepared for the rainy day.

Sleepless nights can perhaps be classed as rainy days. These nights need not be filled with frustrations and murmurings, because God wants us to meditate on Him day and night. *"...His delight is in the law of the LORD; and in his law doth he meditate day and night"* (Psalm 1:2). At times during the night, we may be prompted to pray for someone who is in a difficult or dangerous situation. Our families need intercessory prayer. The aged, our youth, the church, and our government may all be blessed by our prayers. Try praying for each church family and each family member. It is much better to talk to the great Shepherd than to count sheep!

As we grow older, we experience aches and pains unknown to the younger person. It is up to each one of us whether we will allow the rainy days to make us better or bitter. For both husbands and wives, it is important to have a scheduled lifestyle. But in spite of this, we will need to be flexible, because it is God who orders our steps as well as our stops.

God told King Hezekiah, *"Set thine house in order; for thou shalt die, and not live"* (2 Kings 20:1b). God's call to parents today is to keep our homes in order, for we know not what the day may hold. For *"there is but a step between me and death"* (1 Samuel 20:3b).

We as homemakers and wives do our families a favor by planning and keeping our housework up to date if at all possible by cleaning when there is a need; canning and freezing when the produce is ready; keeping the laundry and mending done; in the evening, organizing the house, making it neat and livable; being sensitive to the family's needs; fixing the broken toy; or mending a broken heart.

Always keep in mind that the words you speak may be the last words you utter. Teach the children at every opportunity, because we dare not put off for tomorrow what must be done today. In 2 Peter 3:14b we are told what kind of person God requires: *"Be diligent that ye may be found of him in peace, without spot, and blameless."*

We need not dread or fear the rainy days in life. If we walk with Jesus in the sunshine, He will walk with us through the rainy days!

---

1. Genesis 9:8-17.
2. Hebrews 13:5.
3. Guy Rice Doud, *Molder of Dreams* (Pomona, California: Focus on the Family Publishing, 1990), pp. 46-47.

God's Word must first enter the mind,
before it can enter the heart.

Don't Quit

When things go wrong, as they sometimes will,
When the road you're trudging seems all uphill,
When the funds are low and the debts are high,
And you want to smile, but you have to sigh,
When care is pressing you down a bit,
Rest, if you must—but don't you quit.
Life is queer with its twists and turns,
As every one of us sometimes learns;
And many a failure turns about
When he might have won had he stuck it out.
Don't give up, though the pace seems slow—
You may succeed with another blow.
Success is failure turned inside out—
The silver tint of the clouds of doubt,
And you never can tell just how close you are;
It may be near when it seems afar.
So stick to the fight when you're hardest hit—
It's when things seem worst that you mustn't quit.

Courtesy of Baxter Lane Company, Amarillo, TX, 1975.
Used by permission.

19

Finding the Solution

*O*il on the garage floor again! It had become a daily ordeal to clean up the oil by pouring gasoline on the area and wiping it up with paper towels. But the question remained, Where is the oil coming from? A trip to the mechanic indicated that the car needed a new head gasket. The problem had been solved, the question answered, but there was a price to pay.

Two different accounts in the Bible come to my mind as I think of paying the price to find the solution. One is in 2 Samuel 24. The Bible tells us that David sinned by numbering the people. When David was convicted of his sin, he confessed to God, *"Lo, I have sinned, and I have done wickedly."* He was willing to do what God required, and he paid the price to find the solution. The second account is found in 1 Kings 13. King Jeroboam became angry when the *"man of God"* pointed out his sin. As the king stretched out his hand and pointed his finger, his hand *"dried up, so that he could not pull it in again to him."* Then King Jeroboam entreated the prophet to seek God and pray for his restoration. God answered the prophet's prayer.

Instead of repenting and paying for the solution, he invited the prophet to come to his house. The king wanted to show the prophet kindness by giving him gifts. King Jeroboam was satisfied to continue "cleaning up the spot of oil" rather than repenting of the sin of his rebellious heart.

Not so with King David. He hearkened to the prophet and followed his instructions precisely. David went to Araunah's threshing floor and asked to buy the place to build an altar to make a sacrifice there to God. In the kindness of Araunah's heart, he offered to give King David the place, the oxen, and even the threshing instrument for wood for the offering.[1]

David's answer is a challenge: *"Nay; but I will surely buy it of thee at a price: neither will I offer burnt offerings unto the LORD my God of that which doth cost me nothing"* (2 Samuel 24:24). No wonder David is called a man after God's own heart.[2] When there was sin and failure, he repented and obeyed God wholeheartedly. He refused to sacrifice anything that did not cost him. He found the solution!

In which category do we find ourselves? It is easy to brush over some unkind or harsh remark with the idea that I'll just be careful what I say next time, or I'll do some extra work to mend a broken or hurting relationship. Perhaps even a bouquet of flowers is an attempt to say what words should say, but don't.

In the past two weeks I faced two different encounters that required repentance and restitution. One was a statement I had made that could have hindered God's working in the life of an individual. The second one was provoking a family member to anger. I was deeply convicted both times, and after confession my heart felt so clean and free. Each time there was a price to pay and no amount of "nice kindness" could undo those faults or sins. We do need to allow our spouse and children the freedom to make mistakes, but we need to be seeking continually for the solution. By applying God's Word, we will not make the same mistake time and again.

We should be challenged to grow in our Christian experience. As we grow, the Holy Spirit will minister grace and strength to us in finding the solution and not just being content to occasionally clean up the oil.

In Luke 22:43, the angel ministered to Jesus' need when He faced the Calvary experience. He was strengthened and He was victorious. Therefore, He is our example of victory in everything.

In Jesus we find the price for our victory, and in Jesus we find the solution!

---

1. 2 Samuel 24:21, 22.
2. 1 Samuel 13:14; Acts 13:22.

What God Has Given Me

I haven't a mansion, title, or wealth,
But I have my family and good health.
I have the sun and the sky so blue
And lots of good neighbors too.
I have the moon and the stars so bright
To light up the sky in the darkest night.
I haven't a yacht to sail on the sea,
But I have a husband who loves only me.
So I thank God in heaven above
For giving me these things to love.

—Author unknown

20

Living in the Basement

*O*ur visitors had just arrived. As they stepped inside the door, they took a quick survey and exclaimed, "So you live in the basement!"

Did you know that many people live in the basement in a spiritual sense? It has been said that a person is like a three-story building with a top story, first floor, and a basement. The top story is the spiritual nature, the first floor is the mental nature, and the basement is the physical nature. Many people use their mental nature to feed their physical nature, while their spiritual nature starves.

To be a well-adjusted, balanced person, one must develop the whole person. Overdevelop your physical nature, and you will become even more selfish and ingrown. Overdevelop your mental nature to the exclusion of the spiritual and you will become a skeptic. Few, if any, overdevelop the spiritual nature, for that is hard to do. But if you pay due attention to your spiritual nature, you will give proper attention to your mental and physical well-being as well. Luke 2:52 states that ". . . *Jesus increased in wisdom and stature, and in favor with God and man.*" In this verse, the fourfold nature of man is indicated regarding our Lord. *Wisdom* refers to the mental, *stature* to the physical, *favor with God* to the spiritual, and *man* to the social.

"Study to shew thyself approved unto God, a workman that needeth not to be ashamed, rightly dividing the word of truth" (2 Timothy 2:15).

Confirming our guest's exclamation, we do live in the basement of our house! It is a large, pleasant room. In one corner is a well-supplied kitchen, where many meals have been prepared and served from a beautiful cherry dining room table. On the opposite side of the room is the sewing nook, where the family sewing is done. Also built into this cabinet is the stereo music system—though out of view, it can be enjoyed by all. To the right is a fireplace and a large family room which is carpeted, cozy, and homey. The sun shines through the double windows most of the day, causing the atmosphere to be pleasant and bright. Effort must be taken to view the neighbors or the busy highway, because there are no windows except those toward the woods.

I love living in the basement of our house. It is a place where our family and friends are always welcome. Here we close the door to the outside world. It is cool and comfortable in the summer and pleasantly cozy in the winter. But as much as I love our basement quarters, I am deeply concerned to live well above the basement level spiritually.

You have probably heard these statements: "Tell me what kind of books or papers you read and I will tell you what kind of person you are," or "Let me see your bookshelves and magazine racks because that tells volumes about the family who occupies the house."

Many husbands and wives feed on unwholesome magazines, novels, or sensual sex stories and find themselves becoming discontented with their marriages and homes. To them, the Christian home fails to have the glitter and glamour that appears in their reading world.

For Christians, it should be unthinkable to stoop to such reading and waste God's precious time on such trash. To do so grieves the blessed Holy Spirit. Persons who read such unwholesome material become lean in their souls; worse than that, they are backsliding.

Jeremiah 10:20, 21 gives a picture of such a home.

My tabernacle is spoiled, and all my cords are broken: my children are gone forth of me, and they are not.... For the pastors [parents] *are become brutish, and have not sought the* LORD: *therefore they shall not prosper, and all their flocks* [families] *shall be scattered.*

But since God is a great and wonderful God and "*not willing that any should perish*" (2 Peter 3:9b), He gives us the remedy. If we see the exceeding sinfulness of sin,[1] we get a glimpse of His holiness and we will turn to God for forgiveness. He is always there.

"*O* LORD, *I know that the way of man is not in himself: it is not in man . . . to direct his steps. O* LORD, *correct me, but with judgment . . .*" (Jeremiah 10: 23, 24). "*But put ye on the Lord Jesus Christ, and make not provision for the flesh, to fulfill the lusts thereof.*"[2] As the proper steps are taken to confess and to forsake our sin, God's grace will pardon abundantly. There will be a hunger and thirst for God's Word and will.

Dismiss from your mind the idea that the Bible is a dry, uninteresting book. Such an attitude betrays the fact that you are not becoming acquainted with God's divine and holy Word.

Ask God to enlighten your mind as you read. Make practical application to everyday living, and you will be blessed to find how rich God's Word is and how satisfying to your weary, longing soul.

Yes, God's Word is yours as you read and use it. There is no need to live in the basement spiritually.

---

1. Romans 7:13.
2. Romans 13:14.

I used to pray that God would do this or that.
Now I pray that God will make His will known
to me.

—Mme. Chiang Kai-shek

Courtesy of Baxter Lane Company, Amarillo, TX, 1975.
Used by permission.

Rules for Daily Living

BEGIN THE DAY WITH GOD;
 Kneel down to Him in prayer;
Lift up thy heart to His abode.
 And seek His love to share.

OPEN THE BOOK OF GOD.
 And read a portion there;
That it may hallow all thy thoughts,
 And sweeten all thy care.

GO THROUGH THE DAY WITH GOD,
 Whate'er thy work may be;
Where'er thou art—at home, abroad,
 He still is near to thee.

CONVERSE IN MIND WITH GOD,
 Thy spirit heavenward raise:
Acknowledge every good bestowed,
 And offer grateful praise.

CONCLUDE THE DAY WITH GOD,
 Thy sins to Him confess;
Trust in the Lord's atoning blood,
 And plead His righteousness.

LIE DOWN AT NIGHT WITH GOD,
 Who gives His servants sleep;
And when thou tread'st the vale of death,
 He will guard and keep.

Courtesy of Baxter Lane Company, Amarillo, TX, 1975.
Used by permission.

21

Walk the Chalk Line!

*O*n the way home from church, my mom informed us that Pete and Sara had invited our family to share the following Sunday dinner with them. What excitement and anticipation for us eager children, who always thought it very special when we had an invitation to dinner, especially to Pete and Sara's house!

Our anticipation soared as Sunday approached. On the way, my wise dad looked at his four children in the back seat of our horse-drawn carriage. With sternness in his voice, Dad said, "Children, you walk the chalk line today! Sit still, don't ask for toys, and speak softly when you are spoken to. When we are sitting at the table, eat with your mouth closed, take only one serving, and be sure to eat all your food. Now, remember your manners," Dad added.

Pete and Sara didn't have any children, so their house was always immaculate. No wonder Dad needed to give us these instructions. We were a lively group of children.

In my growing-up years, I was often reminded to "walk the chalk line." Even though it took me years to really appreciate my dad's advice, I am thankful I learned it years ago. God also measured His people once with a straightedge.

A chalk line is a valuable tool in the hand of a builder. He often uses it to give direction for nailing two pieces of material together. *Chalk up,* according to Webster, means "to attain or to achieve."

This is what my dad had in mind when he told me to "walk the chalk line." A good illustration of this is found in Romans 3:20b: *"indeed it is the straightedge of the Law that shows us how crooked we are"* (Phillips).[1]

The Bible also speaks of a plumbline. This is a cord with a weight on one end that serves to determine the vertical alignment of an object. *"Therefore thus saith the LORD; I am returned to Jerusalem with mercies: my house shall be built in it, . . . and a line shall be stretched forth upon Jerusalem"* (Zechariah 1:16). Also in Amos 7:8a, *"the LORD said unto me, Amos, what seest thou? And I said, A plumbline. Then said the Lord, Behold, I will set a plumbline in the midst of my people Israel."* The Greek root word for *plumbline* is "to be narrow." Could it mean a narrow course on which to walk?

Needless to say, "walking the chalk line" is still part of my life. I have often been thankful for a strict dad who insisted that we walk straight, and who also took strong measures if we disobeyed.

Seemingly, some builders today have the idea that the chalk line isn't as important as it was years ago. Could it be possible that the chalk line has lost its significance in the home; therefore, we fail to instill this important aspect in our children's lives?

A disciplined life can be viewed as walking the chalk line. It is described as training that corrects, molds, and perfects the moral character of a person. A disciplined person has a godly perspective, with a vision of much work to be done; thus, there is no time for boredom. The mind is alert and curious to the extent that the person wants to learn all he can in his short life span, to become all God has planned. When there is time on hand, a disciplined person will not be at a loss to know what to do, but will adapt easily to people or solitude. No one is needed to entertain such a person.

To parent disciplined children, we must first be disciplined ourselves. I claim no right to myself, but God is my whole portion. Since more is caught than taught in the disciplined life, it is of great importance that we exemplify by our life what we desire in the lives of our children.

First of all, a disciplined life comes from loving God with all our heart, soul, and mind, then our neighbor as ourselves.[2] Obedience follows love closely. Someone has wisely said, "Prompt obedience is the only obedience that God counts. Slow obedience is no obedience."

Compassion and servitude are the attitudes of a disciplined heart, first to God in sincere thanksgiving and praise, and then to others all around who also will be loved, appreciated, encouraged, and blessed. Contentment, too, is a virtue—not contentment with who we are, but contentment with God's will for our lives. Cheerfulness and gratitude are two additional qualities that prevail in a disciplined life. With these qualities, our speech and way of life will witness of our Christianity. We will also be moderate. We will live within reasonable limits, and calmness and temperance will express our life. We must live consistently in all we do in order to insist that our children "walk the chalk line."

We are certainly living in a day of blurred lines and nondescript grays. In the modern mind, nearly anything is acceptable. We are shocked by the gross immorality around us, but let us not forget that much of this has resulted from a gradual erosion of the disciplined life. If we want good fruit, we must feed the roots. We cannot separate Christian discipline from the reverence and worship that pleases God. If I want my children to walk the chalk line, my challenge is that I must have convictions that show the way of God's chalk line, in God's way, for God's glory.

Obedience is the acid test of a disciplined life. Gold is not changed by a drop of acid, but gold is refined and polished when acid is applied. All other metals either change or corrode. The same is true for the Christian: if he is not gold, he will not be able to "walk God's chalk line."

---

1. J. B. Phillips, *New Testament in Modern English* (New York: MacMillan Company, 1957).
2. Matthew 22:37-39.

Early in his life D. L. Moody made an important discovery regarding success. He spread out his petitions before God and then said, "Thy will be done." It was the sweetest lesson he had learned in the school of obedience: to let God lead and choose for him.

Kitchen Prayer

Bless my little kitchen, Lord,
And light it with Thy Love.
Help me plan and make my meals
From Thy heavenly home above.
Bless our meals with Thy Presence
And warm them with Thy grace;
Watch over me as I do my work,
Washing pots and pans and plates.
The service I am trying to do
Is to make my family content.
So bless my eager efforts, Lord,
And make them heaven sent.

Courtesy of Baxter Lane Company, Amarillo, TX, 1975.
Used by permission.

22

Gather up the Fragments

*H*ere in America we cut a loaf of bread into neat, uniform pieces. But in Central America and in other countries, people break bits off a loaf of bread or cake. I suppose this is how it was done in Palestine when Jesus broke the bread, blessed it, and fed the multitude. It was broken pieces, not slices or leftovers.

What a comfort and encouragement to read the account in John 6. Jesus not only blessed the bread, but He broke it and shared it with the people. Therefore, every morsel He had blessed was, in His sight, worth gathering up for later use!

Do we at times feel like odds and ends of loaves, not worthy to be called anything? We need not despair. As we become broken pieces that He can bless, our lives will be useful. Even the "crumbs" of our lives will not be lost. If my life is broken when given to Jesus, it will become pieces that will feed many, whereas a loaf will satisfy only one. It is of interest that the writers of the four Gospels were inspired to record the account of one boy whose loaves and fish fed the multitude.[1]

Zechariah 4:10 tells us not to despise the day of small things. Later in the verse the reason is given. We dare not overlook small things because *"the eyes of the LORD . . . run to and fro through the whole earth."* If small things were important in Zechariah's day, how much more in our day? God's eye does behold everything! It is so important to be sensitive to little things so that nothing is lost.

It was a typical Sunday morning. The rest of the family was in the car, ready to go to church. As usual, I waited until everyone else went outside; then I made my round to see that the time bake was turned on to the proper temperature. I turned off a light, switched the fan on low, and pushed the doorknob to lock the door. A quick glance around the kitchen reminded me that someone had left his Bible on the table, and the Amish Mennonite Aid newsletters were left on the sewing machine cabinet. My arms were full of various items that needed to be taken along to church that morning. As I took my place in the front seat of the car, one of the girls said, "Mom gathered up the fragments." As I pondered the statement, I was challenged anew that as mothers we often are called upon to gather up the pieces. We are to work behind the scenes to keep the household organized and to keep things ticking.

In the day of modern conveniences, it is very easy to throw away little things. Rather than repairing the worn-out timer on the electric range, we lightly toss the range aside and buy a new one. After all, it's 15 years old. Perhaps Mr. Jones would really be glad for it. He probably wouldn't even use the timer. The hoe or shovel handle is broken, and, we reason, it takes too long to chisel out the old handle and replace it with a new one. We'll just buy a brand new shovel instead. The lawn mower just isn't fast enough, so we become discontented, wishing for a better mower rather than enjoying walking more slowly and beholding the beauty of a freshly mowed lawn. A glance in the refrigerator reminds me there are leftovers that need to be used, but instead I would rather fix a meal from fresh foods. So out the door goes food enough to feed a hungry child in a war-torn country. We should not throw out, but repair where we can and fix food from our abundance. We need to acknowledge that our overabundance at times makes us despise little, insignificant things.

We often lose little opportunities to teach our children by example that we are stewards of God's many blessings and that *"the* LORD *is in his holy temple . . . ; his eyes behold, his eyelids try, the children of men"* (Psalm 11:4). Let us take the challenge to teach our children the blessing of contentment and the blessing of making good use of little things. Our husbands also need encouragement to be sensitive to save and be a good steward of the many blessings God has entrusted to us. God does not measure us by success but by faithfulness in little things. There is a real blessing and fulfillment in being a mother who is willing to *"gather up the fragments that remain, that nothing be lost"* (John 6:12b).

---

1. In addition to John 6, this story is recorded in Matthew 14:13-21; Mark 6:30-44; and Luke 9:10-17.

The Joys of a Mother

I've done an angel's work today!
Yes, such an honor came my way.
Real angel's work! And, lest you doubt it,
I'm going to tell you all about it.
Well, first I cooked. It was so nice
To plan the pies, stewed fruit, and rice.
God sent His angel once to make
Cakes for a poor wayfarer's sake.
But, just today He honored me
And sent the task my way, you see.
Then, while I tidied up the place,
Gave every knob a radiant face,
Back of my mind this thought would lurk,
That I was still at angel's work,
Putting away coats and dresses,
And moving small unsightliness.
For, oh! 'tis such a lovesome thing,
Just straightening out and freshening.
And after that I washed a few
Small woolly garments, old not new,
Things I had rubbed and rinsed before,
Quite forty times, or even more.
And as I hung them on the line,
I thought what God-like work was mine!
To cleanse—ah, me! to wash out stains
Till not a single speck remains.
So, later in the day 'twas sweet
To sit and rest my tired feet
Mending the clothes, and plan out, too,
How to make old things into new.
For surely 'tis an angel's way
To put things right from day to day,
To find thin places and repair
The glad rags and the sturdy wear.
Since wear and tear must surely be
On this side of Eternity.
I'm feeling very blessed to say
I've done an angel's work today!

—*Author unknown*

Courtesy of Sword of the Lord Publishers, Murfreesboro, TN, 1969.
Used by permission.

23

The Joy of Housecleaning

*H*omemaking is said to be a biblical lifestyle and a joy to the Christian wife and mother. It is within this realm that she finds joy in housecleaning.

Webster describes *joy* as "expressing delight, feeling successful." I believe every wife does find a bit of pleasure when she has accomplished the task of cleaning house.

Proverbs 24:3, 4 gives us a picture of a clean, God-fearing home. *"Through wisdom is an house builded; and by understanding it is established: And by knowledge shall the chambers be filled with all precious and pleasant riches."*

Since *"the fear of the LORD is the beginning of knowledge"* (Proverbs 1:7a), the home must be built on godly principles. Understanding is a much-needed ingredient in the home (Proverbs 4:7). This indicates prudence, insight, and intelligence. Knowledge is gained through the senses; therefore, God's principles are in circulation. Only then can the rooms be filled with precious memories. Moments are temporary, but memories last a lifetime. There is something inviting, warm, and endearing about such a home. It need not be immaculate, but will be modestly clean. With small children, the house will not stay perfectly in order, but it can still be clean even though toys clutter the floor.

I have often been grateful for a mother who could organize. She taught her three girls to get work done, even though many times I pushed things into corners or tried to hide unpleasant tasks. But when I got married, I knew it depended on me to get my work done. I didn't have much time to debate whether I wanted to do it or whether it was necessary. I knew I had to do my work or suffer the consequences of an untidy home.

Many choices must be made daily, and often people are tempted to think, "I don't like to do the cleaning, so I'll do it later." But we have no promise of the morrow.[1] It is always a good policy to do the cleaning or other jobs promptly, without procrastinating.

I have learned the joy of housecleaning, but I am indebted to Ella May Miller, speaker on the former *Heart to Heart* broadcast and author of many books for homemakers, whose interesting and noble writings encouraged me to put God first, my family next, and to give them all I have. Many of her thoughts, quotes, and writings have molded my thinking and lifestyle to become all God planned for our family. I am deeply grateful to God and Ella May. It is for this reason that I want to encourage all wives, and especially young wives, in the importance of living with a purpose and zeal even in the so-called "lowly" tasks of housecleaning.

When our first waking thoughts are of God, it can be with gratitude to our heavenly Father that we can "rise and shine"! Perhaps a phrase of song comes to mind. During the warm season, it often is the song of the whippoorwill that alerts me to the beginning of a brand-new day. Dressing with a neat and clean appearance can be pleasantly attractive to our families.

The first room that should be kept clean and attractive is the bedroom. Make the bed wrinkle free; straighten up the room so everything is in place; then close the door.

It should be our privilege to spend some time in Bible reading and prayer, if not the first thing in the morning, perhaps at a later time that suits better. We should also be concerned that our husbands and children have a nutritious breakfast and family worship before the family goes their various ways. After breakfast, the kitchen should be cleaned up: dishes washed and put into the cabinet with the counters, stove, and refrigerator clean and in order.

Many women find it important to write down goals they would like to achieve for a day or a week. It's a good policy to get the unpleasant tasks done first. Try timing yourself, setting goals, and you will be surprised and blessed to find the tasks were not so dreadful. Neither did time slip away from you. Again, the slogan "Work well planned is work half done" is very true! Some people spend so much time planning and talking about how they want to perform that they find no time left for their performance.

Another room that can be kept pleasant and clean is the living room. A wife feels much better about herself (and I think this is a part of joy) if there is organization in the living room, with it kept orderly for family and guests alike. If possible, the living room door could be closed. Children will soon know where the limits are. But mothers must be consistent; they dare not demand that the door be closed one day, then allow the children to romp and play in the living room the next day.

The children's bedrooms should also be kept modestly clean and orderly. Children can be taught to make their beds neatly with their mother's help. It is also a blessing to work together, over and over again, helping the children to do a better job than the time before.

I did not allow our children to play or keep their toys in their bedrooms because I wanted them to play where I was working. When young children develop the habit of playing where Mother works, as they grow older they will not be content to go to their bedroom to play. Even though it takes longer for a mother to do her work this way, it is such a blessing to have the children where she can hear and join in the conversation. As the children play or "help" their mother, it affords ample time for discussion and questions that mothers are best suited to answer.

Another reason for children playing in the kitchen is that we do not entertain our visitors in the bedroom, so why should our children entertain their guests in the bedroom? There were times when our guests' children asked about playing in the bedroom, and I kindly but firmly said "no." I am sure many unwholesome conversations and actions can be avoided when we consistently live by God's principles. Table games can be played on the kitchen table, or children can learn to sit and listen to what the older ones are saying.

We must teach our children to be trustworthy. We must make sure they are worthy of trust before we send them out into an untrustworthy and dishonest society. It takes time and effort, and we cannot afford to allow our children to play by themselves where Mother is not aware of what is going on. Since children are full of folly,[2] they need constant care and guidance.

There is a thought afloat that "quality time is more important than quantity time," but this has not proven to be true! Quality and quantity are of equal importance. Many questions and ideas that make up the child cannot be related and shared in short order. Mothers must be there and listen. That way she knows what her children are thinking and can give proper guidance. It is at this age that open communication begins and good relationships are built that last a lifetime. Our children developed an appreciation for an orderly bedroom. It was there that they slept rather than played; therefore, they found it frustrating when there was disorder.

There is a great need today to instill a diligent and honest spirit in our children. Many times children are more content to help in their own way than to be told to run and play. I'm sure it takes longer to get things done when our children are underfoot, but what is the hurry? We are raising God's children for eternal purposes! Certainly it is important to get our work done and our house clean, but since our spiritual and material phases of life are so interwoven, we are what we are and that is what our children will become. Therefore, we must keep our priorities straight.

The bathroom is another very important room to keep clean. Imagine living a hundred years ago, using outdoor facilities. Here we are with all the modern conveniences! Frequently these rooms are not kept as clean and sanitary as they could be. It does not take long to scrub the toilet often to prevent repulsive odors. Children need to be taught to use these facilities correctly. Little boys can be taught to "sink the boat" by putting a small piece of toilet tissue into the toilet for their aim. Children must be taught to wash their hands and flush the toilet, even if they must stand on the toilet seat or use a small step stool to reach the sink. Faucets can be marked to distinguish between hot and cold. Perhaps our first thought is, "I don't have time," but it is these little areas that bring joy. Our task as mothers is not getting the work done ourselves, but sharing the load. Through this, our children are taught responsibility.

Spring and fall housecleaning is another duty that can be viewed with dread. Perhaps you feel it is not needful, or maybe once a year is sufficient for you. One mother has a goal to clean thoroughly one room each month; for another, it's done whenever she feels like it; and still another would rather rummage through crowded closets to find what she is looking for. Nevertheless, I find it is important to go through the whole house in the spring and fall. Since our wedding anniversary is the middle of March and my birthday is the middle of September, I have these dates as my goal for completion of housecleaning. Usually, during the month of February, I do the necessary painting or wallpaper hanging and clean out every nook and closet; then in the fall I go through everything a bit more quickly.

For years, I tried to prepare my family for these "house-shaking" events because no one fancied the disruptions. One spring I decided I'd try another method. I quietly went through the rooms, cleaning one room at a time, being more careful not to upset too much at once. One day when I went to town to rent the steam vacuum, my husband and son were so surprised; they hadn't even been aware of what I was doing. So after that success, I no longer tried to prepare them, but quietly went about my work. I believe it was more joyful for all involved.

When we accept the role of homemaking, we accept many unknown events that will take place, such as cooking, cleaning, and perhaps many lowly, unnoticed tasks. In doing these, we are living in obedience to God because true faithfulness brings true joy and fulfillment.

Our senses must be sharp so we are aware of what is going on around us. If we want to prevent mishaps, we must teach and train consistently day in and day out. Isaiah 28:10 reminds us that it must be *"precept upon precept; line upon line."* Deuteronomy 6:7, 8 and Deuteronomy 11:19-21 remind us of nearly the same message. There is never a vacation from teaching and training our children.

It is easy to fail to detect problems soon enough. We choose which we will be doing: either we'll be busy preventing errors, or we'll have a lot of repairing to do in broken relationships and communications. Good relationships bring joy and gladness to housecleaning. When we fail, we spend our latter years lamenting, "If only I had. . . ." Doing things God's way means being aware that an ounce of prevention is worth a pound of cure! When we truly love our children as God loves us, we will be deeply concerned about their spiritual well-being. Therefore, we will deal sternly with sin, keeping their good in mind.

It is of utmost importance to be aware that as we clean the house, we also need to check and cleanse our heart. Every thought and attitude must be pure and clean in order to have a blessed abode for our Lord and Savior Jesus Christ. Just as we desire Jesus to be the center of our homes, so He must first dwell in our pure hearts. Jesus is really the key to a joyful life of housecleaning.

---

1. James 4:14.
2. Proverbs 22:15.

A Mother From A–Z

A ttitudes of joy make her home a pleasant place to be.

B lessings are many as she balances the budget and plans for the family.

C heerfulness is her lot as she oversees her household tasks.

D uties, whether great or small, are all fulfilled by diligence.

E nthusiasm marks her labor in the garden as she plans for the winter meals.

F aithfully she cans and freezes for the family and friends alike.

G ratitude is in her heart, even though she is weary to the bone.

H ealth is important to her, both physical and spiritual.

I ndustry provides a channel for her energies.

J ustice and mercy go hand in hand as she disciplines the children.

K nowledge of the Scripture is her guide for life.

L ove, the greatest virtue, makes duty a delight.

M eekness describes her way; she is not proud or boastful.

N ever does she cease to pray and nurse her family.

O bedience to her Father commands obedience from her children.

P atiently she teaches, line upon line, here and there a little.

Q uietness and confidence in the Lord is her strength.

R ight living brings her life above reproach.

S inging lifts hers and the family's spirits, thereby imparting blessings.

T rust in the Lord is her motto.

U nderstanding is what she prays for daily.

V igilance is needed to keep her household in order.

W aiting on the Lord, she finds answers to the children's questions.

'X perience brings many joys as she mothers her children from total dependence to independence.

Y ielding not to temptation, she does not compare herself with others.

Z eal for the Lord characterizes her service to her family and others.

Does this describe you?

24

Retracing My Steps

I tiptoed down the hall. What a moment of quietness, of awesome relief, for both babies were asleep. How I longed for those quiet times when I could be alone with God and sort out my priorities.

This illustrates the daily grind of life most young mothers face. Because of urgent demands, finding time to be alone with God is very difficult.

My desire was to grow in holiness and become better acquainted with God's holy Word. The only way to accomplish this, we usually decide, is to spend more time with God. But there is another aspect. The reality of becoming holy does not happen only as we read the Bible and pray; it happens in everyday life as we, by His strength and grace, apply His Word and obediently act upon it.

As a very young, immature Christian in my early twenties, I found myself an overwhelmed mother of a tiny baby and a toddler. Knowing God was still my real concern, but how could I get to know Him better?

God always has a plan, even though He may not allow circumstances to change or adjustments and schedules to become lighter. He chose to use my babies as His instruments in changing my life. He taught me lessons that would help me progress toward growth.

God started where it hurt most—with self. Nothing hinders fellowship with God more than self-centeredness. I thought I had died to self, but motherhood was my proving ground.

Toddlers and babies have ways of being demanding. Consequently, I soon learned that selfishness must go or sanity will. Sacrifice becomes the way of a mother's life. I soon learned I must focus on others, not on self. Dying to self is not easy, but the rewards of freedom from self-centeredness make it well worth the effort. Dying to self teaches many lessons, and one of them is servanthood. We must learn to orient our lives to meet the needs of others. For a mother, servanthood is an absolute necessity. Mothers do not have time to think, "Shall I serve or not?" They just serve! There is no sleeping late in the morning, no quiet evening to pursue a hobby, no reading for relaxation. Each day consists of feeding, bathing, cleaning up the house, and caring for husband and children. By evening, sleep is often a welcome relief from a busy day.

Children are good teachers of endurance and patience. This does not consist of one day of hard work or one early morning rising, but rather comprises years of interruptions and demands. I was forced to develop self-discipline and diligence. Day after day, it is the same routine, and often without recognition or reward. But the discipline and diligence I gained in the process are valued results.

Humility, too, is learned. Many times I failed in being patient and kind. By failing in these areas I failed God. Facing God after such failures only drew me to Him for strength, help, and wisdom. Had I focused only on the moment, I possibly would have despaired. But, instead, as I labored, I recognized that this was my God-given lot in life, and each day I enjoyed His blessing through the lives of our children.

My desire to grow in Christ's likeness was granted and, too, God blessed me with a burden also to help the children grow to shoulder responsibility and to be aware of His requirements in obedience and respect. When we have the proper perspective, we will use our possessions to build our children. We will not use our children to increase our possessions. Then, too, in our concern to provide a pleasant atmosphere for our children, we need continually to remind ourselves that we dare not fail the Lord by failing our children. Nor do we want to fail our children by failing to keep God first in our priorities.

It helped me to remember that, as mothers, we are models who should recommend nothing to our children that we have not already tried and found to be what we believe is best. One such example is living a consistent, disciplined life. Through this we teach the importance of endurance. We are not called to an easy life, but to endure hardness by God's grace.[1]

Now here I am, retracing my steps after many years of mothering. Someone nobly said, "Once a mother, always a mother." My ears still catch those cries, "Mama, Mama!" Even though these cries call for other mothers, I'm still reminded of my struggles, failures, victories, joys, and all the happiness little children bring.

My desire is to encourage and pray for young mothers as I observe them caring for their babies and children. There are times when I notice a mother who looks weary, or one who needs to mete out discipline. Or I see a mother getting up from her chair numbers of times to make sure her orders are carried out. These mothers need all the encouragement they can get to be consistent.

Motherhood usually begins early in life, while one may still be an immature, floundering, young Christian. I am thankful God planned it that way. It is with a grateful heart that I observe our daughter-in-law. She consistently keeps her eyes on her young son and has her ears tuned to hear. At times it seems as if she has eyes in the back of her head; very few misdeeds escape her attention.

This is the way God planned it! God gives mothers grace to be consistent, even when they are tired, because their goal has far-reaching effects. As we do our best, we have the confidence that God will do the rest.

This, then, can be our prayer:

Build me children, O Lord, strong enough to face themselves when they are afraid. May they be honest and humble and gentle.

Build me children whose wishbone will not replace their backbone, children who know You. To know You as Lord and Savior is the foundation of true knowledge and wisdom.

Lead them, I pray, not in paths of ease and comfort; but, under the stress and difficulties of life, spur them on by challenges. Here let them learn compassion for those who fail.

Build me children whose hearts are pure and clean, whose goals are high, children who master themselves by Your help; who learn to laugh, yet don't forget how to weep; who reach into the future; yet never ignore the past.

And after these things are theirs, I pray give them humility so that they may always remember the simplicity of true greatness, be open to true wisdom, and in meekness find true strength.

Then I, their mother, by Your grace may dare to whisper, "I have not lived in vain."

---

1. 2 Timothy 2:3.

When I Have Time

When I have time, so many things I'll do
To make life happier and much more fair
For those whose lives are crowded now with care.
I'll help to lift them from their low despair,
*   When I have time.*

When I have time, the friend I love so well
Shall know no more these weary toiling days;
I'll lead her feet in pleasant paths always,
And cheer her heart with words of sweetest praise,
*   When I have time.*

When you have time! The friend you hold so dear
May be beyond the reach of your intent;
May never know that you so kindly meant
To fill her life with love and sweet content,
*   When you had time.*

Now is the time! Ah, friend, no longer wait
To scatter loving smiles and words of cheer
To those around whose lives are now so drear.
They may not meet you in the coming year—
*   Now is the time!*

Courtesy of Sword of the Lord Publishers, Murfreesboro, TN, 1969.
Used by permission.

25

Working Myself Out of a Job

A woman's life consists of continual change. Therefore, it is so important that we learn contentment. Paul's testimony in Philippians 4:11b is, *"For I have learned, in whatsoever state I am, therewith to be content."*

A woman does not enjoy stress, because stress takes its toll. First, she is a bride, learning the basics of relating to her husband. Then she becomes a mother of small children who need much care and attention. In the next phase, she finds herself involved in school lessons and school-related activities. Then, suddenly, she is aware that the children do not need that constant care they once demanded. She may feel threatened by her children's independence, but this should not be, and will not be if she has the proper concept of life.

In this stage of life, she could make the mistake of believing she is no longer needed and withdraw into a shell of self-pity. But her children need her now more than ever; however, they need her in a different way. Earlier, she instructed and they followed carefully. Her position now is to be available to listen, to encourage, and to lend a helping hand when needed. She must be there and be interested. Otherwise, she may lose the valuable art of communication with her family at a very crucial point. The teenager must know there is a praying mother who is interceding with God for her children, one who listens without lecturing or "preaching." It is in this phase of life that she comes to the stark realization that she is slowly working herself out of a constant job of mothering.

In order to face graciously the stress of many changes, she must have a proper concept of short- and long-term goals. She must also find fulfillment and contentment because God is leading. Then the stress will not become overwhelming.

One real blessing is that God has wisely planned for husband and wife to parent their children and unitedly face the changes that are sure to come. Since their joy and fulfillment is not found in going places, in material possessions, or in circumstances, they become richer and more content as they follow Christ and grow up in Him. *"That Christ may dwell in your hearts by faith; that ye, being rooted and grounded in love . . ."* (Ephesians 3:17). This is the only way to accept changes and grow older cheerfully.

Mother and Father together must remember that whether their children spend eternity in heaven or in hell, whether they rise to success or sink to failure, and whether they find fulfillment or live in confusion depends largely on their home training. The example of parents sets the stage for their children's well-being. What an awesome responsibility to accept that our children's security, the noblest issue in their lives, revolves around the center of parental interest. One of the greatest tragedies of this age is the unmistakable indifference on the part of parents toward this basic truth.

Parents must recognize that they are ordained by God to scrutinize the demands of this life in order to meet their children's spiritual and physical needs. If parents are preoccupied with business or social obligations, some of these should be dropped, because the collapse of parental authority is one of the major factors in the staggering rise of delinquency. It is, therefore, imperative that God's plan for the family be followed closely and carefully. Every phase of life is ordered by God, and He has our good in mind.

King Solomon gives us the key to victorious living. In Ecclesiastes 12, we are admonished to remember our Creator in our youth, before we become involved in so many things that draw our attention away from God.

Hannah had a proper concept of working herself out of a job. She prayed for a son and God answered her prayer. She promised to give him back to God all the days of his life. She recognized that God had only lent Samuel to her for a short time, to nurture and train for God's service.[1]

Moses' parents are another example of diligent parenting that paid dividends. They had the privilege of teaching their young son for several years before the king's daughter adopted him as her son.[2] Hebrews 11:24-26 gives Moses' testimony. He chose to suffer affliction with God's people rather than to enjoy the temporary pleasures of Egypt. Moses kept the reward of heaven in view. He had a proper concept of life and eternity because his parents dared to instill principles into his young life. These principles developed into conviction that lasted all his life.

Mrs. Zebedee was a typical mother! She had high and noble goals for her two sons, James and John. Her encounter with Jesus is recorded in Matthew 20:20-22. She requested that her sons sit on Jesus' right and left in His kingdom. Perhaps we are too much like Mrs. Zebedee. We pray selfishly that our children fill some prominent position, or we encourage them to marry some popular individual rather than pray for God's will to be done, encouraging them to be faithful wherever God calls. Our responsibility is to teach by our life and example that Jesus deserves all our allegiance. Only as we die to self can our lives be blessed and fulfilled.

John the Baptist showed us by his example how to work ourselves out of a job. He was sent by God to prepare the way for Jesus. John said, *"He must increase, but I must decrease"* (John 3:30). As we see our children grow in their Christian life and develop convictions in the wisdom and knowledge of God, we must step aside gradually and allow them to become personally responsible and accountable to God. Again, we find that the constant job of parenting lessens as the children grow up. Never, though, do we arrive at a plateau that releases us from the responsibility of encouragement, counsel, prayer, and intercession for them. Like Job, we must pray and ask God's continual blessing, protection, and forgiveness upon them.[3]

Through every phase of life, women must nourish their souls with good works. They can find joy and peace in solitude, strength in prayer, and wisdom by reading God's Word. We must always seek to reflect God's radiance even in our busy lives. Perhaps someone asks, "Who has time for all this?" Our older years will be only as rich and joyful and fulfilling as we make the day today! We usually find time to do the things we want to do most. Why else do we have all these labor-saving devices in our homes? Often we fail to realize that we will be forever what we are becoming today. Instead of taking time to do what we should, we say, "Someday things will be different. Someday I'll have more time. Sometime when the children are grown, I'll do this or that."

Years ago I observed a certain older sister who was a good example for me as a young mother. Her dedication to God and her family was outstanding. She had a large family and enjoyed each one. Later, when she and her husband were in their forties, God blessed them with two more children. All too soon, these two grew up and left home. As she was going through this stage in life, I noticed she no longer seemed to be the joyful mother she had been; instead, stress and a nervous state took its toll.

As mothers, we need to keep in mind that life does continually change. It is very needful to plan for our future, even when our days do not contain enough hours to get the things done that need our attention. We must keep in mind that we are really working ourselves out of the job of mothering. Therefore, it is imperative to plan, or at least to pray, and be open to prepare for when we are older and life is less demanding.

It is important to have some other interest through which we can find fulfillment in years to come. Some find real fulfillment in returning to the classroom as a teacher. Some enjoy being more involved in volunteer work in the church or community. Others have returned to their former career of nursing. Some need to spend more time with their elderly parents. There is a great need for writing and art for church papers. Many avenues are opened for the Christian woman who has been faithful within the four walls of her home. I keep reminding myself that we must always have time for our husbands, children, and grandchildren. When we seek God's will in areas such as this, God has promised that we shall find His plan and His blessing even in this stage of life.

Some time ago, a friend of mine shared that an older friend encouraged her and her husband to leave the needs at home and in the church saying, "You need to enjoy yourself and relax. You need to get away. You owe it to yourself."

The wise man, Solomon, has good counsel for this older friend.

> *Vanity of vanities, saith the Preacher, vanity of vanities; all is vanity. What profit hath a* [woman] *of all* [her] *labour which* [she] *taketh under the sun?* (Ecclesiastes 1:2, 3, paraphrase).

In the following verses, he describes a life characterized by "going in circles."

> *One generation passeth away, and another generation cometh. . . . The sun also ariseth, and the sun goeth down. . . . The wind goeth toward the south, and turneth about unto the north; it whirleth about continually; . . . the wind returneth . . . to his circuits. . . . The eye is not satisfied with seeing, nor the ear filled with hearing* (Ecclesiastes 1:4-8).

King Solomon allowed his selfish nature to dictate his life. Therefore, he was not fulfilled, but rather empty, because he went in circles. The carnal person is never satisfied; he always craves something new, something exciting and more thrilling. King Solomon experienced everything his heart desired, and in his older age he confessed it to be vanity of vanities and even vexation of spirit. It is no wonder that 12 chapters later Solomon pleads that all people remember now their Creator in their youth (Ecclesiastes 12:1).

My friend was frustrated. She did not feel she needed to "get away." She loved and was concerned about her family and also the well-being of the church. She was a good example of a mother who was finding joy and fulfillment right at home.

In order to do so, we must continually live by Proverbs 3:5, 6: *"Trust in the* LORD *with all thine heart; and lean not unto thine own understanding. In all thy ways acknowledge him, and he shall direct thy paths."* We dare not allow the world in which we live to dictate our thinking or make us discontented with God's many blessings in the Christian family.

If we expect our older age to be a blessing, we must be found living for God now. We should not wait until our hair turns gray, then try quickly to become what God desires. We must be found in God's righteousness today, so God can bless our latter years as well. *"The hoary head is a crown of glory, if it be found in the way of righteousness"* (Proverbs 16:31).

Job 5:26 compares growing older to a ripened shock of grain. Age is inevitable, yet God leaves the choice with each of us whether we will grow older cheerfully and joyfully, or whether we will try to deny our age. For the Christian woman, it is a blessing to realize that God has so graciously led her safely thus far, and that by His grace she will continue to enjoy living in the realm God has so wisely designed for her.

Life also can be likened to fruit trees. Every year the grower expects more and better fruit. So it is with God: every year He expects His children to yield more and richer fruit. Like the grower, God patiently cares for us and permits joys and sorrows to make us more refined and mature. If we view aging from a human perspective, we will be discontented and complaining. Psalm 90:12 tells us to number our days, not our years. We must live one day at a time. As we live by His principles, He will provide daily strength and grace for us to live enthusiastically for Him. If we accept each day as a gift from God, we will be controlled by His grace to live for His glory.

Is growing older dreadful? Never.

> Challenging? Yes.
>
> Changing? Often.
>
> Humbling? Occasionally.
>
> Rewarding? Eternally.

But the key to living realistically is:

> to give graciously,
>
> adapt willingly,
>
> trust fearlessly,
>
> rejoice daily.

"So the LORD blessed the latter end of Job more than his beginning" (Job 42:12a). It is God's perfect will that we enjoy each day allotted to us. By God's grace, our latter end, like Job's, can be more blessed.

---

1. 1 Samuel 1, 2.
2. Exodus 2:1-10.
3. Job 1:5.

Looking for the Sunrise

I'm not looking for the sunset
 As the swift years come and go;
I am looking for the sunrise
 And the golden morning glow,
Where the light of heaven's glory
 Will break forth upon my sight,
In the land that knows no sunset
 Nor the darkness of the night.

I'm not going down the pathway
 Toward the setting of the sun,
Where the shadows ever deepen
 When the day at last is done.
I am walking up the hillside
 Where the sunshine lights the way
To the glory of the sunrise
 Of God's never-ending day.

I'm not going down, but upward,
 And the path is never dim,
For the day grows ever brighter
 As I journey on with Him.
So my eyes are on the hilltops,
 Waiting for the sun to rise—
Waiting for the invitation
 To the home beyond the skies.

—Author unknown

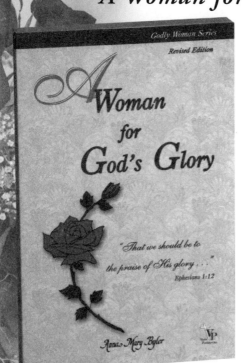

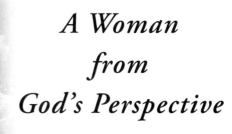

A Woman from God's Perspective

Two people view the same facts but reach opposite conclusions. One focuses on the lacerating, stabbing pain of the moment, whereas the other transforms the same circumstances into radiant accomplishment. A pearl, after all, is "wondrous beauty wrapped around trouble." Such a splendid response is possible only if one trusts each life incident to God's all-inclusive point of view. Anna Mary Byler shows how this divine perspective is worked out in the daunting responsibilities and magnificent opportunities of a woman's calling.

Paperback - 176 pages - $5.99 - ISBN 0971705461

To order, use the order form in the back of this book

Order Form

To order, send this completed order form to:
Vision Publishers
P.O. Box 190
Harrisonburg, VA 22803
Phone: 877/488-0901
Fax: 540/437-1969
e-mail: visionpubl@ntelos.net

_____   _____
Name   Date

_____   _____
Mailing Address   Phone

_____
City   State   Zip

A Woman by God's Grace   Quantity _____ x $5.99 each = _____

A Woman for God's Glory   Quantity _____ x $6.99 each = _____

A Woman from God's Perspective Quantity _____ x $5.99 each = _____

Price _____

Ohio residents add tax rate for the county in which you reside _____

Virginia residents add 5% sales tax _____

Shipping and Handling __**$4.50**__

Grand Total _____

All Payments in US Dollars

❏ Check #_____
❏ Money Order
❏ MasterCard   ❏ Visa

Card # |__|__|__|__| |__|__|__|__| |__|__|__|__| |__|__|__|__|

Exp. Date |__|__|__|__|

Thank you for your order!

For a complete listing of our books,
write for our catalog.

Bookstore inquiries welcome

Order Form

To order, send this completed order form to:
Vision Publishers
P.O. Box 190
Harrisonburg, VA 22803
Phone: 877/488-0901
Fax: 540/437-1969
e-mail: visionpubl@ntelos.net

_____ _____
Name   Date

_____ _____
Mailing Address   Phone

_____
City   State   Zip

A Woman by God's Grace   Quantity ____ x $5.99 each = _____

A Woman for God's Glory   Quantity ____ x $6.99 each = _____

A Woman from God's Perspective Quantity ____ x $5.99 each = _____

Price _____

Ohio residents add tax rate for the county in which you reside _____

Virginia residents add 5% sales tax _____

Shipping and Handling __**$4.50**__

Grand Total _____

All Payments in US Dollars

❑ Check #_____
❑ Money Order
❑ MasterCard   ❑ Visa

Card # _|_|_|_|_| _|_|_|_|_| _|_|_|_|_| _|_|_|_|_|

Exp. Date _|_|_|_|_|

Thank you for your order!

For a complete listing of our books, write for our catalog.

Bookstore inquiries welcome

You Can Find Our Books at These Stores:

CALIFORNIA
Squaw Valley
  Sequoia Christian Books
  559/332-2606

COLORADO
Fruita
  Grand Valley Dry Goods
  970/858-1268

FLORIDA
Miami
  Alpha and Omega
  305/273-1263
Orlando
  Borders Books and Music
  407/826-8912

GEORGIA
Glennville
  Vision Bookstore
  912/654-4086
Montezuma
  The Family Book Shop
  478/472-5166

ILLINOIS
Arthur
  Clearview Fabrics and Books
  217/543-9091
  Miller's Dry Goods
  175-E County Road 50-N
Ava
  Pineview Books
  584 Bollman Road

INDIANA
Goshen
  Country Christian Bookstore
  574/862-2691
  Miller's Country Store
  574/642-3861

  R And B's Kuntry Store
  574/825-0191
  Shady Walnut Grocery
  574/862-2368
Grabill
  Graber's Bookstore
  260/627-2882
LaGrange
  Pathway Bookstore
  2580 North 250 West
Middlebury
  F and L Country Store
  574/825-7513
  Laura's Fabrics
  55140 County Road 43
Nappanee
  Little Nook Bookstore
  574/642-1347
Odon
  Dutch Pantry
  812/636-7922
  Schrock's Kountry Korner
  812/636-7842
Shipshewana
  E and S Sales
  260/768-4736
Wakarusa
  Maranatha Christian Bookstore
  574/862-4332

IOWA
Carson
  Refining Fires Books
  712/484-2214
Kalona
  Friendship Bookstore
  2357 540th Street SW

KANSAS
Hutchinson
  Gospel Book Store
  620/662-2875

**Our books may also be found on many
Choice Books bookracks and Lantern Books bookracks**

Moundridge
Gospel Publishers
620/345-2532

KENTUCKY
Harrodsburg
Family Bookstore
859/865-4545
Manchester
Lighthouse Ministries
606/599-0607
Stephensport
Martin's Bookstore
270/547-4206

LOUISIANA
Belle Chasse
Good News Bookstore
504/394-3087

MARYLAND
Grantsville
Shady Grove Market and Fabrics
301/895-5660
Hagerstown
J. Millers Gospel Store
240/675-0383
Landover
Integrity Church Bookstore
301/322-3311
Oakland
Countryside Books and More
301/334-3318
Silver Spring
Potomac Adventist Bookstore
301/572-0700
Union Bridge
Hege's Catalog Store
410/775-7643

MICHIGAN
Burr Oak
Chupp's Herbs and Fabric
269/659-3950

Charlotte
Meadow Ridge Woodcrafts LLC
517/543-8680
Clare
Colonville Country Store
989/386-8686
Fremont
Helping Hand Home
231/924-0041
Holton
Country Cottage Bookstore
231/821-0261
Sears
Hillview Books and Fabric
231/734-3394
Snover
Country View Store
989/635-3764

MINNESOTA
Lansing
Maranatha Bible School
507/433-6642

MISSOURI
Advance
Troyer's Grocery
573/722-3406
La Russell
Schrock's Kountry Korner
417/246-5351
Rutledge
Zimmerman's Store
660/883-5766
St. Louis
The Home School Sampler
314/835-0863
Seymour
Byler Supply & Country Store
417/935-4522
Shelbyville
Windmill Ridge Bulk Foods
4100 Highway T

**Our books may also be found on many
Choice Books bookracks and Lantern Books bookracks**

Versailles
Excelsior Bookstore
573/378-1925
Weatherby
Country Variety Store
816/449-2932
Windsor
Rural Windsor Books and
Variety
660/647-2705

NEW MEXICO
Farmington
Lamp and Light Publishers
505/632-3521

NEW YORK
Dunkirk
The Book Nook
716/366-0685
Seneca Falls
Sauder's Store
315/568-2673

NORTH CAROLINA
Greensboro
Borders Books and Music
336/218-0662
Raleigh
Borders Books and Music #365
919/755-9424

NORTH DAKOTA
Mylo
Lighthouse Bookstore
701/656-3331

OKLAHOMA
Miami
Eicher's Country Store
918/540-1871

OHIO
Berlin
Gospel Book Store
330/893-2523

Christian Aid Ministries
330/893-2428
Brinkhaven
Little Cottage Books
740/824-4849
Carbon Hill
Messiah Bible School
740/753-3571
Dalton
Little Country Store
330/828-8411
Fredricksburg
Faith-View Books
330/674-4129
Hopewell
Four Winds Bookstore
740/454-7990
Leetonia
Tinkling Spring Country Store
330/482-4592
Mesopotamia
Eli Miller's Leather Shop
440/693-4448
Middlefield
S and E Country Store
440/2347
Millersburg
Country Furniture & Bookstore
330/893-4455
Plain City
Deeper Life Bookstore
614/873-1199
Seaman
Keim Family Market
937/386-9995
Sugarcreek
J S R Fabric and Shoes
330/852-2721

The Gospel Shop
330/852-4223

Troyer's Bargain Store
2101 County Road 70

**Our books may also be found on many
Choice Books bookracks and Lantern Books bookracks**

OREGON
Estacada
Bechtel Books
530/630-4606
Halsey
Shoppe of Shalom
541/369-2369

PENNSYLVANIA
Amberson
Scroll Publishing Co.
717/349-7033
Belleville
Yoder's Gospel Book Store
717/483-6697
Chambersburg
Burkholder Fabrics
717/369-3155

Pearson's Pasttimes
717/267-1415
Denver
Weaver's Store, Inc.
717/445-6791
Ephrata
Clay Book Store
717/733-7253

Conestoga Bookstore
717/354-0475

Home Messenger Library &
Bookstore
717/351-0218

Ken's Educational Joys
717/351-8347
Gordonville
Ridgeview Bookstore
717/768-7484
Greencastle
Country Dry Goods
717/593-9661
Guys Mills
Christian Learning Resource
814/789-4769

Leola
Conestoga Valley Books
717/656-8824
Lewisburg
Crossroads Gift and Bookstore
570/522-0536
McVeytown
Penn Valley Christian Retreat
717/899-5000
Meadville
Gingerich Books and Notions
814/425-2835
Mount Joy
Mummau's Christian Bookstore
717/653-6112
Myerstown
Witmer's Clothing
717/866-6845
Newville
Corner Store
717/776-4336

Rocky View Bookstore
717/776-7987
Parkesburg
Brookside Bookstore
717/692-4759
Quarryville
Countryside Bargains
717/528-2360
Shippensburg
Mt. Rock Bookstore
717/530-5726
Springboro
Chupp's Country Cupboard
814/587-3678
Stoystown
Kountry Pantry
814/629-1588

SOUTH CAROLINA
Barnwell
The Genesis Store
803/541-6109

**Our books may also be found on many
Choice Books bookracks and Lantern Books bookracks**

North Charleston
World Harvest Ministries
843/554-7960
Summerville
Manna Christian Bookstore
843/873-4221
Sumter
Anointed Word Christian Bookstore
803/494-9894

TENNESSEE
Crossville
MZL English Book Ministry
931/277-3686

Troyer's Country Cupboard
931/277-5886
Deer Lodge
Mt. Zion Literature Ministry
931/863-8183
Paris
Millers Country Store
731/644-7535
Sparta
Valley View Country Store
931/738-5465

TEXAS
Kemp
Heritage Market and Bakery
903/498-3366
Seminole
Nancy's Country Store
432/758-9162

VIRGINIA
Bristow
The Lighthouse Books
703/530-9039
Dayton
Books of Merit
540/879-2628

Mole Hill Books & More
540/867-5928
Rocky Cedars Enterprises
540/879-9714
Harrisonburg
Christian Light Publications
540/434-0768
McDowell
Sugar Tree Country Store
540/396-3469
Rapidan
Faith Lions
540/672-3566
Woodbridge
Mennonite Maidens
703/622-3018

VERMONT
Bennington
Christian Book Store
802/447-0198

WASHINGTON
North Bonneville
Moore Foundation
800/891-5255

WEST VIRGINIA
Renick
Yoders' Select Books
304/772-4153

WISCONSIN
Dalton
Mishler's Country Store
West 5115 Barry Rd.
Loyal
Homesewn Garments
715/255-8059
South Wayne
Pilgrims Pantry
608/439-1064

**Our books may also be found on many
Choice Books bookracks and Lantern Books bookracks**

CANADA

ALBERTA
Cleardale
Cleardale Christian Bookstore
780/685-2582

BRITISH COLUMBIA
Burns Lake
Wildwood Bibles and Books
250/698-7451
Montney
Janice Martin Books
250/327-3231

MANITOBA
Arborg
Sunshine Christian Books
204/364-3135

ONTARIO
Aylmer
Mennomex
519/773-2002

Brunner
Country Cousins
519/595-4277

Lighthouse Books
519/656-3400
Floradale
Hillcrest Home Baking and Dry
Goods
519/669-1381
Linwood
Living Waters Christian Book-
store
519/698-1198
Mount Forest
Shady Lawn Books
519/323-2830
Newton
Zehr's Country Market
519/595-7585

**Our books may also be found on many
Choice Books bookracks and Lantern Books bookracks**